I0815010

FASCINATION SEASIDE LIVING

BRAUN

FASCINATION SEASIDE LIVING

ARCHITECTURE AND DESIGN

BRAUN

CHRIS VAN UFFELEN

CONTENTS

CONTENTS

A Caspar David Friedrich
The Monk by the Sea, 1808–1810
Oil/canvas
110 cm × 171.5 cm
Alte Nationalgalerie, Berlin

A

Seaside Living means living at the interface of the elements earth, water and air. But it also means dealing architecturally with the conditions of nature in its solid, liquid and gaseous state of matter.

The fascination of living at the seaside means incorporating these manifestations of nature into the architectural design, both structurally and emotionally. After all, it is almost always the longing for the place that determines the choice of a particular building site: The search for a fascinating symbiosis between human and man-made habitat and the grandeur of untamed nature. Ever since Edmund Burke's "Enquiry into the Origin of our Ideas of the Sublime and Beautiful" in 1756, man has seen more in nature than just the condition of his existence, and has felt in awe at its diversity, infinity and boundlessness. The heroic landscape compositions of Classical painting and the idyllic landscapes of Romanticism still bear witness to this new perception of nature around 1800. For some it was the grandeur and potential violence of nature, for others it was the intimate personal experience that defined the experience of nature. Even today, the special atmosphere of living at the seaside moves between these two poles. Both can be found in the sound of the waves rolling gently onto the shore and in the cooling breeze blowing off the water. The whisper of the wind represents the longing for freedom; the surf testifies to the endless coming and going; the salty air tastes of nature.

Glass fronts and open floor plans create a seamless connection between indoor and outdoor spaces and the ocean. Natural light, which quickly changes the mood as it streams in through the windows, integrates the rooms with nature. Only the rooms facing away from the beach are often more enclosed as retreats. The living spaces, on the other hand, are designed to reflect the freedom of the beach. Open floor plans not only promote a sense of ease, but also allow for natural ventilation, which is especially beneficial in warm coastal areas. However, the location also presents challenges such as the salt content of the air, high humidity, and the constant influence of wind and sand. In this context, the choice of materials and construction methods play a crucial role. Robust, corrosion-resistant materials that can withstand the effects of salt water are essential to ensure the longevity of the structure. Sea level rise and heavy storms are also factors to consider when building for living at the seaside.

Ultimately, however, none of these issues and concerns can detract from the seaside as a place of longing. Et in Arcadia ego – I too (am or was) in Arcadia.

FORESHORE HOUSE

A

LANDSCAPE DESIGN
Trish Dobson
INTERIOR DESIGN
Hare & Klein
AREA
452 m^2
YEAR
2020
PHOTOGRAPHY
Simon Wood
www.swphotography.net.au

Foreshore House sits on the eastern shore of Pittwater in Sydney's Northern Beaches area, providing breathtaking 180-degree water views from Scotland to Lion Island. This residence is the result of a major renovation of an existing building that had suffered storm damage. Keeping the footprint and envelope of the existing dwelling, the house was extensively remodeled to accommodate a large family. The exposed timber frame of the original building was reimagined as a laminated timber portal frame for the new upper floor. Foreshore House's location on a steep, wedge-shaped site was a construction challenge. Retaining walls and a new boat shed with a rooftop spa were built within the high tide zone. Materials such as compressed fiber cement siding, copper rainwater fixtures, sandstone flagstones, and spotted gum windows and doors were selected for their durability in coastal conditions.

A House and boat shed, viewed from the water
B First floor kitchen and dining area

B

C

C Boat shed rooftop with timber spa
D Lightweight floating roof
E House façade made of materials suitable for coastal conditions

D E

F

G

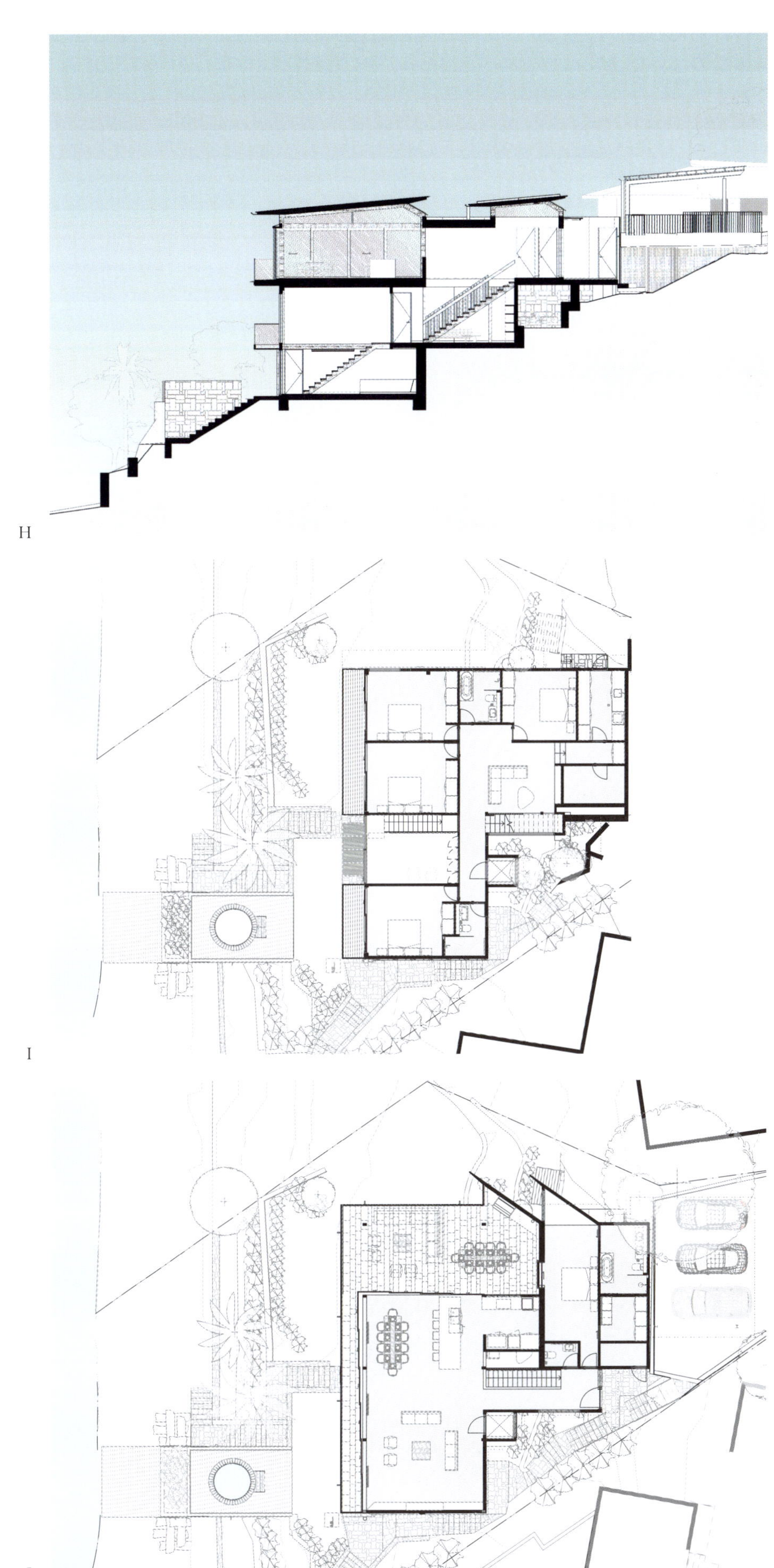

H

I

J

F Dining area with panoramic view
G Stacking doors open the living areas to the foreshore
H Section
I Ground floor plan
J First floor plan

CASA FLY

A

CASA FLY

LANDSCAPE DESIGN
Mallorca Eden Jardin
AREA
304.5 m^2
YEAR
2020
PHOTOGRAPHY
Tomeu Canyellas
www.tomeucanyellas.com

Casa Fly is in harmony with traditional Mallorcan architecture, using materials such as stone from a local quarry, along with local techniques and empirical principles. The stone façade is based on a typical design that can be found all over the island as fences or retaining walls, constructed using a traditional dry technique called Pedra en sec. This local design has been declared Intangible Cultural Heritage of Humanity by Unesco in 2018. The massive façade helps to keep the house cool in the summer months and accumulates heat in the winter. The windows are set deeply into the walls in order to create shade from the concrete slabs. The folding wooden shutters are another natural heat prevention. Spaces in between the lamellas allow air to circulate even when the shutters are closed. The stone façade, in combination with the lime plaster Estuco de cal, flows continuously into the interior.

A Outdoor dining space overlooking the sea framed by trees
B Entrance façade complemented by a gate and green accents

B

CASA FLY

C South façade based on Pedra en sec with terraces surrounding infinity pool

C

D

E

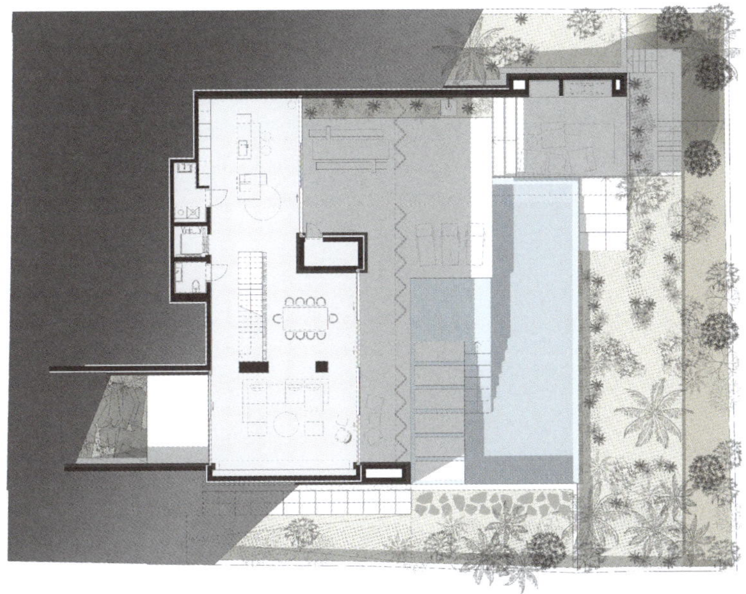

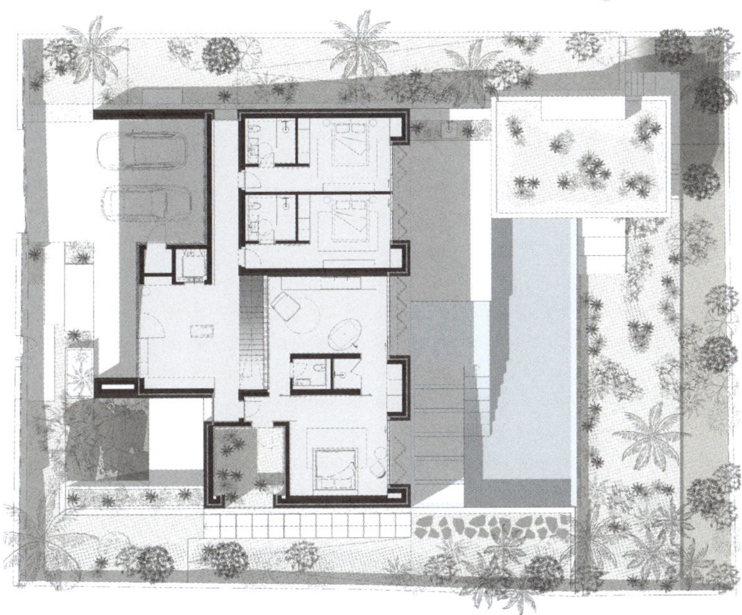

F G

H

D Front view of south façade with pushed back windows and open shutters
E Interior dining space with handcrafted ceramic drop-lights
F Ground floor plan
G First floor plan
H Entry space featuring greenery and wooden pivot door

22

LIGHT HOUSE

A

23

LIGHT HOUSE

AGGER
DENMARK

CLIENT
Søren Sarup
AREA
153 m²
YEAR
2018
PHOTOGRAPHY
Tina Steffansen
www.studio55.dk

Light House is situated in the western part of Denmark at the North Sea. It is surrounded by a landscape of dune heaths and lakes. These as well as the soft northern light, the view and the sound of the wind in the reed were elements of inspiration for the A-frame house. It consists of two very different but complementary structures: A horizontal rectangular body with large windows, and a vertical slate covered triangular body. The unique quality of the house is the close contact between inside and outside. Wide windows frame the landscape around the vacation home and the hidden window frames create a visual continuation to the terrace areas outside. Light House was designed in the Nordic design tradition, in which the proximity to nature, the use of light and the airy openness create a unique architectural experience. Warm wood surfaces and Danish furniture classics create a calm and relaxed atmosphere.

A Bathroom with panoramic view
B Exterior view

B

C D

E

C Frontal exterior view
D Main entrance and terrace
E Child's bedroom on the ground floor
F Master bedroom
G Kitchen

F

G

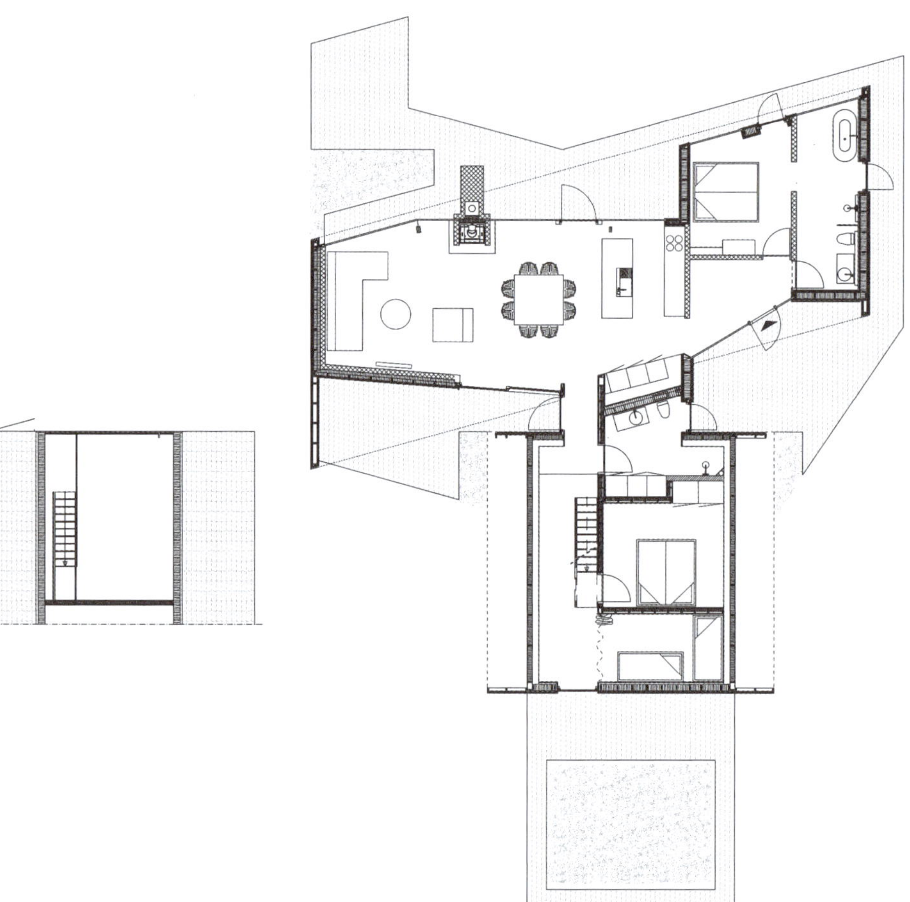

H

I

H Ground floor plan
I Staircase leading to first floor
J Living room with panoramic view
K Bathroom with panoramic view

J

K

DUNE HOUSE

A

29 DUNE HOUSE

TE ARAI
NEW ZEALAND

LANDSCAPE DESIGN
Xanthe White Landscape Design
INTERIOR DESIGN
Intext Design
AREA
600 m²
YEAR
2021
PHOTOGRAPHY
Simon Devitt
www.simondevitt.com

Dune House is a vacation home in a coastal golf resort north of Auckland. The site offers magnificent views to the ocean beyond and across the golf course to the wider natural landscape. However, the building's design must also respond to the harsh conditions of the dune. It is built low into the site, with flat timber roofs cantilevering out to form generous covered terraces. Stone-clad columns anchor the horizontal planes of the roofs to the ground and frame the panoramic views. The floor plan divides the house into separate wings for living and sleeping. A Moroccan limestone masonry was used to mimic the tone of the sand, combined with oiled cedar for both the wall and ceiling planes. Color accents are provided by rusted Corten steel and the blue of the pool. The landscaping responds to the dune environment with desert plants, reinforcing the architecture's references to mid-century American Modernism.

A Pool deck with ocean view
B Exterior view with surrounding sand dunes

B

C

D

E

F

C Living area with views of the surrounding landscape
D Cactus garden
E Dining and kitchen area
F En-suite shower with ocean view

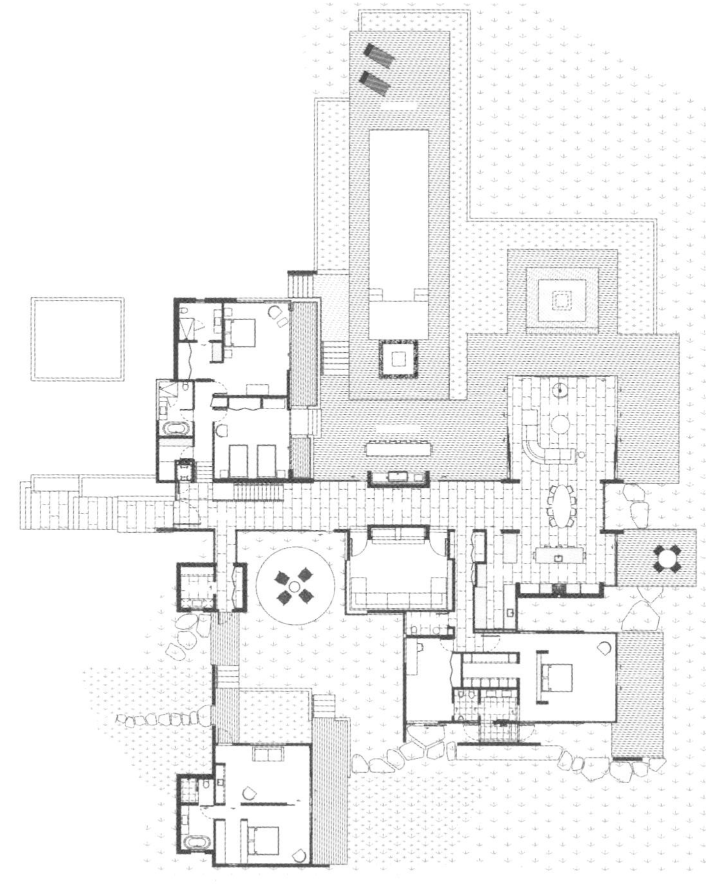

G

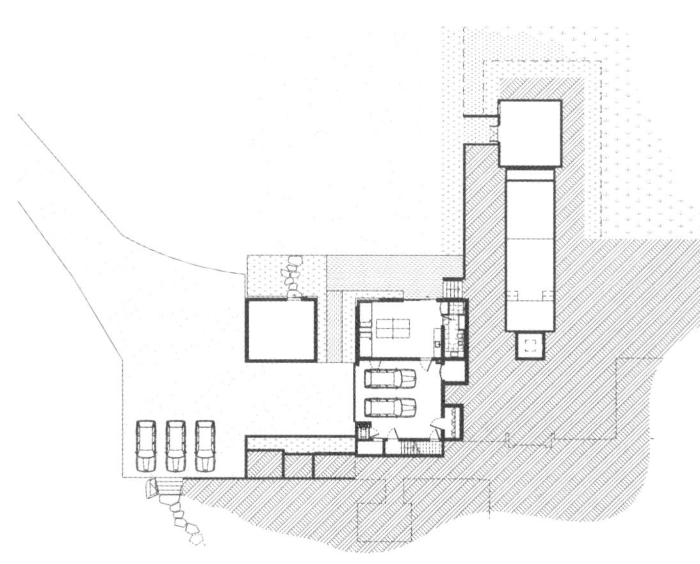

H

G Ground floor plan
H Lower level plan
I Detail of exterior entrance stairs

THE SEASIDE VILLA

A

35 THE SEASIDE VILLA

AARHUS
DENMARK

CLIENT
Jørgen Danielsen
AREA
500 m^2
YEAR
2020
PHOTOGRAPHY
Mikkel Frost

The Seaside Villa is situated at Aarhus Bay, providing stunning ocean views and showcasing a unique roof design. Depending on the coastal weather conditions and the viewpoint, the house takes on a different shape. The space-defining undulating roof with varying heights creates a dynamic sculptural appearance both indoors and outdoors. Eaves reduce the thermal stress on the central space's glass façades and create generous, covered outdoor areas protected from the elements. The exterior features classic Danish bricks that are rich in tactility, referencing the beach with preserved sand residue. Warm wooden details contrast the interior with a welcoming atmosphere. Norwegian slate covers all floors, creating cohesion between indoor and outdoor spaces. The villa harmoniously blends contemporary expression with traditional materials, forming a visually appealing piece of architecture.

A Bayfront façade with undulating roof
B The villa takes on a different shape depending on the point of view

B

C Living area
D North façade
E Two-story hallway with staircase and Norwegian slate floors

C

D

E

F

F South façade at night
G Entrance area at night
H Elevations
I Ground floor plan

G

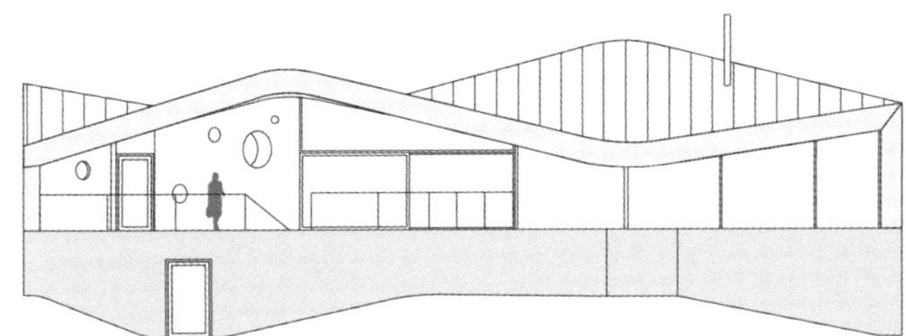

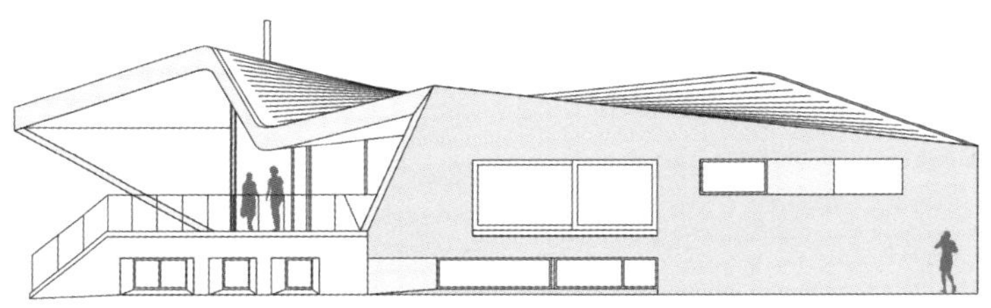

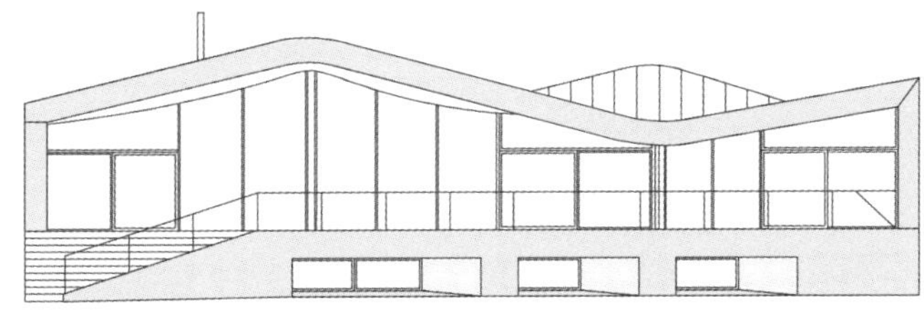

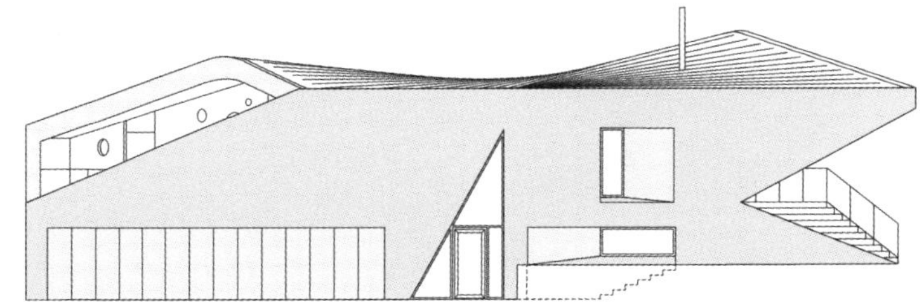

H

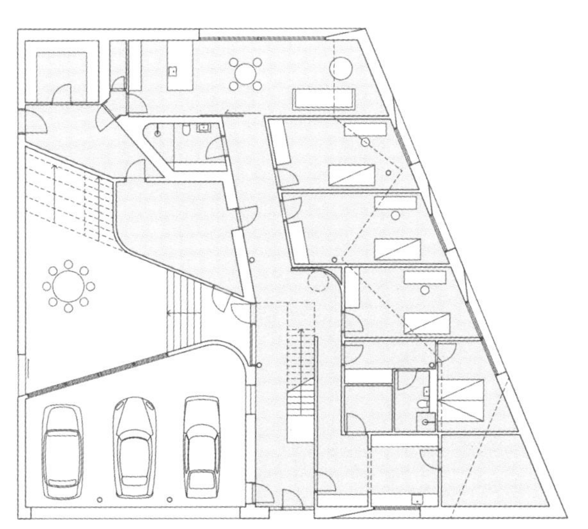

I

FABIO MAZZEO ARCHITECTS

VILLA IN SARDINIA

A

41

VILLA IN SARDINIA

SARDINIA
ITALY

INTERIOR DESIGN
Exclusiva
AREA
1,200 m²
YEAR
2016
PHOTOGRAPHY
Massimo Camplone Photo Studio
www.massimocamplone.it

Villa in Sardinia is located on the Costa Smeralda, on a promontory sculpted by the wind. This is the result of an interplay of continuous references that emphasize the links between the building and its natural environment, as well as the balance between aesthetics, quality and functionality. The building unfolds on three levels, in harmonious symbiosis with the terraced garden and the panoramic infinity pool, whose austerity is softened by the presence of the old olive trees. The building is a perfect example of contemporary residential architecture in an exceptional setting. If travertine is the unifying theme that dominates the exterior, the interiors are an expression of attention to detail, where precious materials, unique objects and artistic decorations create an elegant atmosphere. The main entrance catches the eye with its portal, which like a textured painting, evokes a panorama of sails.

A External pool area
B Living room

B

C

D

C External view
D Master dressing room
E Lobby

F

G

H

I

J

F TV room
G Entrance hall
H Aerial view
I Main entrance
J Pool view

EAST END HOUSE

A

EAST END HOUSE

LONG ISLAND
NY, USA

LANDSCAPE DESIGN
Edmund Hollander Design
AREA
278 m^2
YEAR
2019
PHOTOGRAPHY
Albert Vecerka-Esto
www.esto.com

Perched on a bluff overlooking the water, this house on Long Island's East End was designed as a serene, year-round retreat. In summer living spaces open outward to the landscape, capturing cool breezes and lapping waves, while in winter they turn inward to a cozy two-sided fireplace and warm wood paneling. Wide cantilevered overhangs create dramatic external rooms while providing additional shade from the summer sun. The house settles into its natural environment, prioritizing new and old growth trees, outdoor living spaces, and views while using its low profile to minimize its presence on the site. A familiar regional palette of red cedar, copper, and bluestone serves the passive house construction strategies incorporated, which include thick insulated framing, a continuously insulated envelope, energy-recovery ventilation and an environmentally beneficial green roof.

A Living area
B Dining area

B

C House façade and surrounding nature

C

50

D

E F

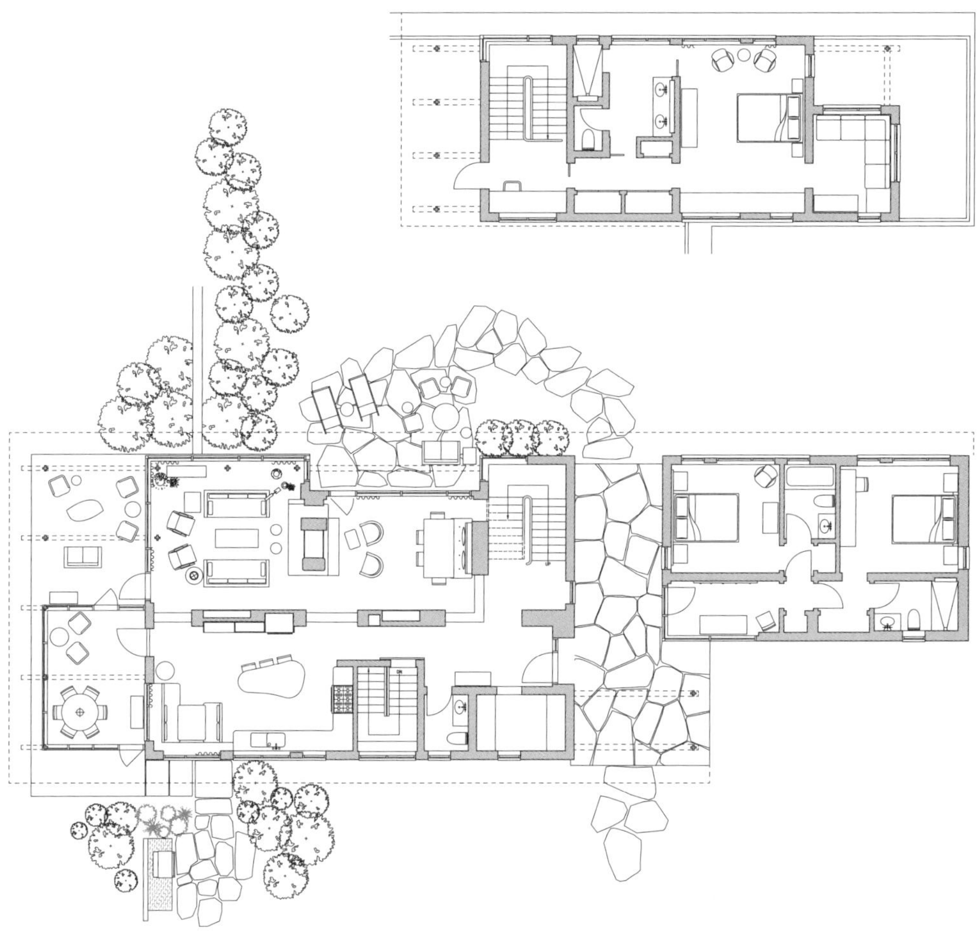

G

D Screened porch
E Master bedroom
F Dining area detail
G First and ground floor

52

ALDO BEACH HOUSE

A

53

ALDO BEACH HOUSE

HOOD CANAL
WA, USA

AREA
188 m^2
YEAR
2019
PHOTOGRAPHY
Andrew Pogue
www.andrewpogue.com

Aldo Beach House transforms a 1940s beach house into a new multi-generational home – doubling the livable area while lightly touching the delicate ecology of the waterfront. Two shifting wings hover over the hillside and beach supported by thin steel columns and pin piles. Due to the complex constraints of the shoreline exemption, the architects kept to the existing footprint. The modernized beach house includes the original two-bedroom structure for an expanded program of two new bedrooms, two bathrooms, and flex space. The gabled roof has been removed. The new wings of the house create a layering of community and privacy through guest bedrooms for friends, a bunk room and play area for kids, and an outdoor kitchen and deck for communal meals with neighbors. Native plantings and drought tolerant species were brought in to mitigate site disturbance and increase the ecological function of the site.

A Wing hovering over decks on pillars
B View to lake-deck beneath extension
C Deck, lake and reflection

B C

D

E F

G H

D Stairs made of concrete and Corten steel
E Lattice
F Wooden stairs
G Small terrace
H Large bedroom window

I J

K

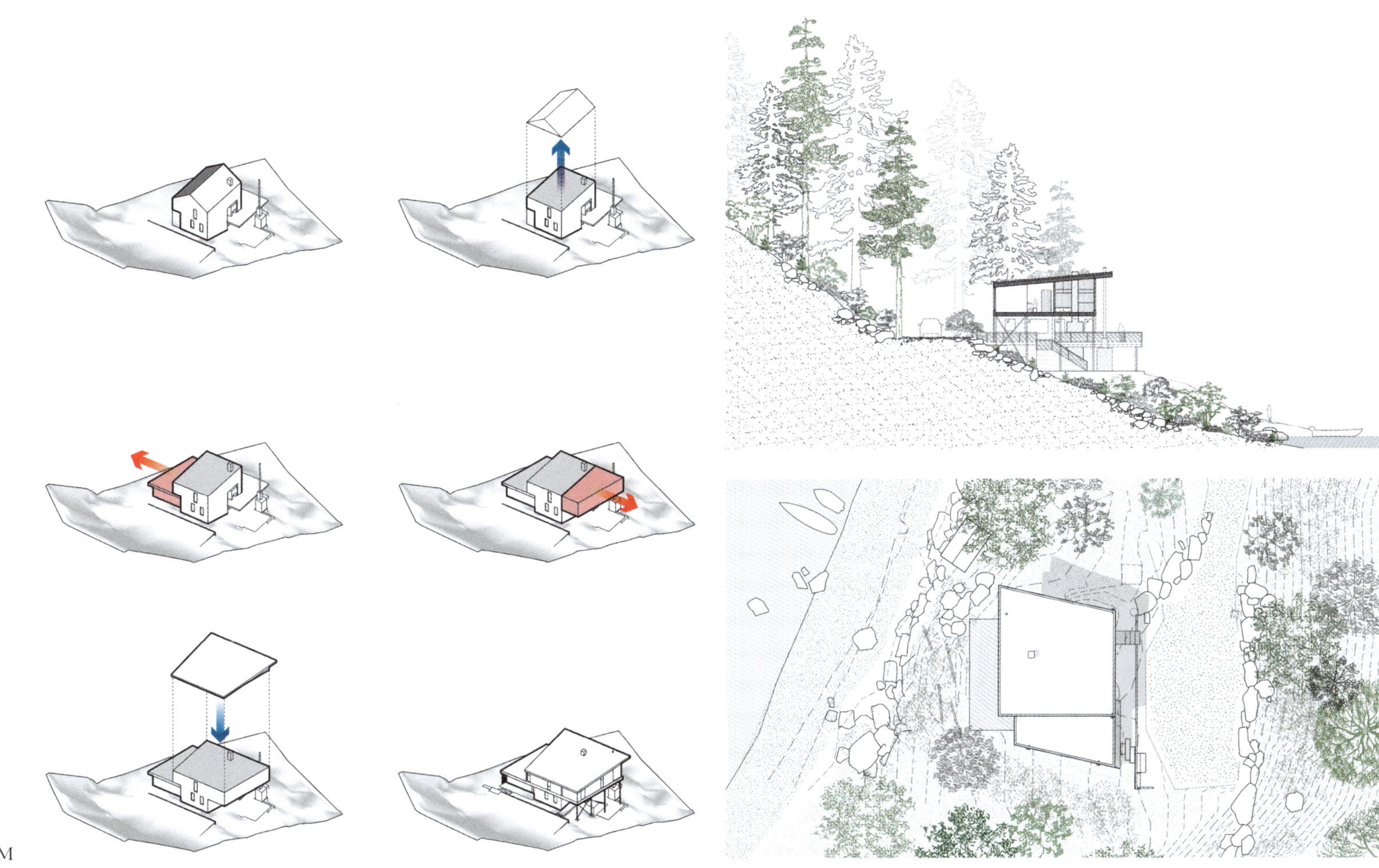

L M

I View from study
J Bedroom upper floor
K Kitchen main floor
L Design process
M Section and site plan

VILLA AT LAKE CONSTANCE

A

59 VILLA AT LAKE CONSTANCE

LAKE CONSTANCE
GERMANY

AREA
300 m²
YEAR
2018
PHOTOGRAPHY
Tom Philippi (A, B, G, K, L)
www.tomphilippi.de
Dorothea Craven (C, D, E, F)
www.dorotheacraven.de

The design of the Villa at Lake Constance drew inspiration from the site's shore context, aiming to showcase water as a tangible and moving element. The new ground and upper floor were added to the existing building, of which the basement and indoor pool were retained. The basic form of this villa reads as a right-angled cube, which presents as two airy boxes balanced atop one another. The first floor rests on the east and west wings and creates the illusion of floating. Large shadow gaps between the east and west wings accentuate this effect. The design makes for a spacious living area on the ground floor with completely glazed façades on either side. This connects the terrace on the south side, with its view of the lake, to the courtyard and swimming pool on the north side. The glass elements are deliberately set back from the edge of the building, allowing the lake to be observed from many angles.

A North façade
B Two-story living area lake view

B

C D

E F

G

C Gallery view to the living area
D Dining area and kitchen
E Living area detail
F Gallery and wall detail
G South façade night view

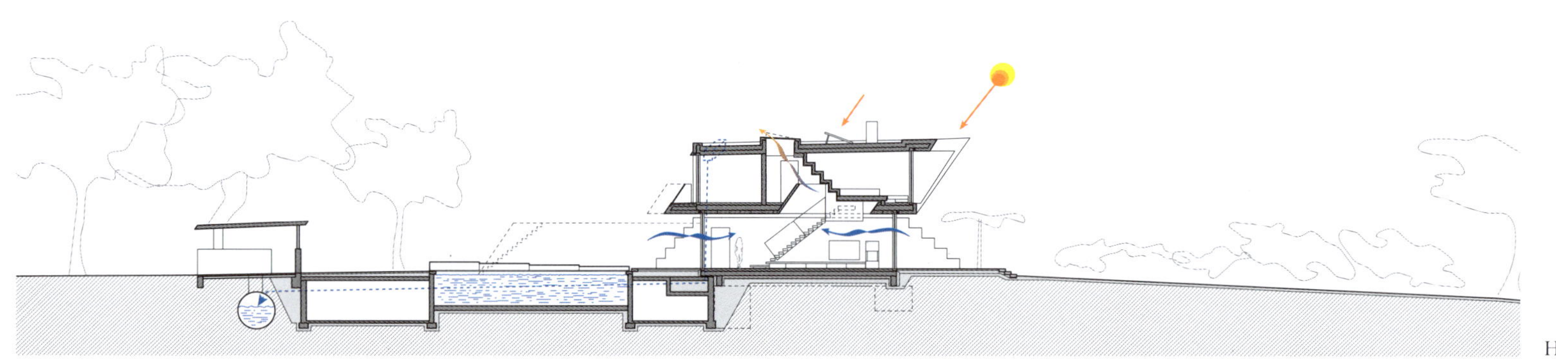

H

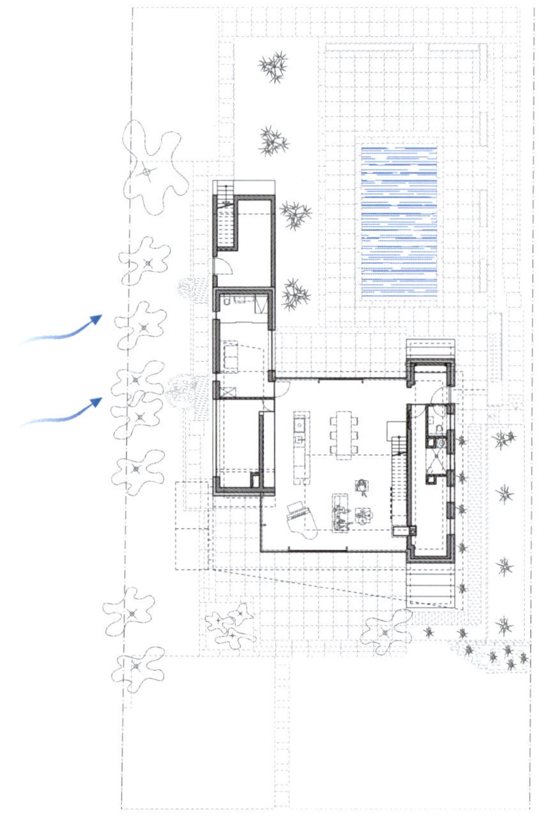

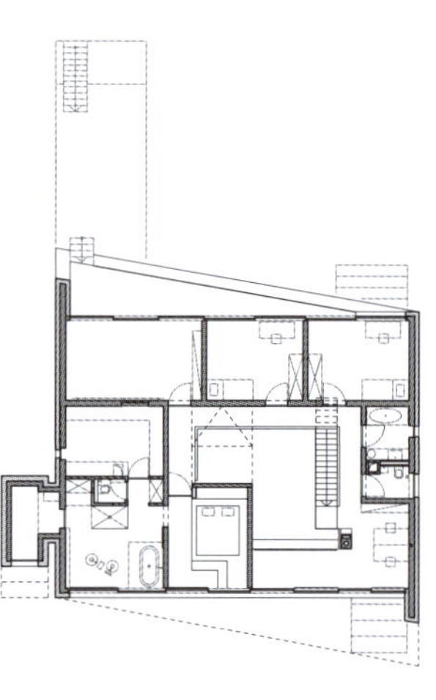

I J

K

L

H Cross section
I Ground floor plan
J First floor plan
K South façade
L Bathroom lake view

CRUACHAN BEAG

A

CRUACHAN BEAG

COILLEAG, ISLE OF ERISKAY, UNITED KINGDOM

CLIENT
Andy Laverty & Family
AREA
30 m^2
YEAR
2020
PHOTOGRAPHY
Alex James (A, B, D, F, G)
BARD (C, E)

The project utilized an existing stone ruin on the Outer Hebrides, Scotland, to form a space to dine, to rest and to bathe, whilst maximizing the beautiful outlook. It was considered from the outset how the building could be designed to improve with the influence of time. An entrance sequence containing several 90-degree turns was the initial design generator. A small area of the ruin is left open, creating a sheltered court to form an entrance and a place to sit, store logs, and decompress from the outside world. From here the first turn leads to the kitchenette, followed by a diagonal to the view. The building is firmly rooted in its site. The sense of space and outlook opens the tiny house up and makes it seem spacious. It is now another onlooker to its immense surroundings with a renewed purpose.

A Western wall details
B View from the east towards Lingay

B

C

C View from Prince's Bay beach
D Play of light and shadow

D

E F

G

E Adaptable interior
F Space to rest
G Internal view towards ferry terminal
H Site plan
I Floor plan

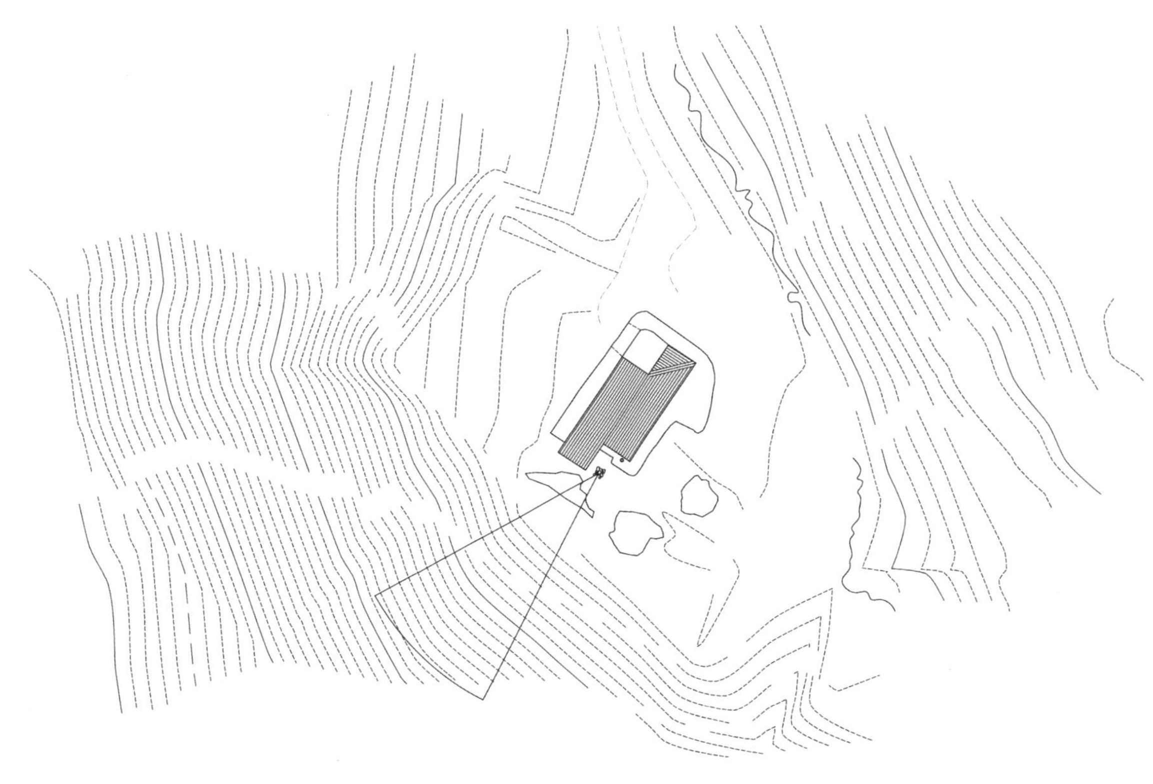

H

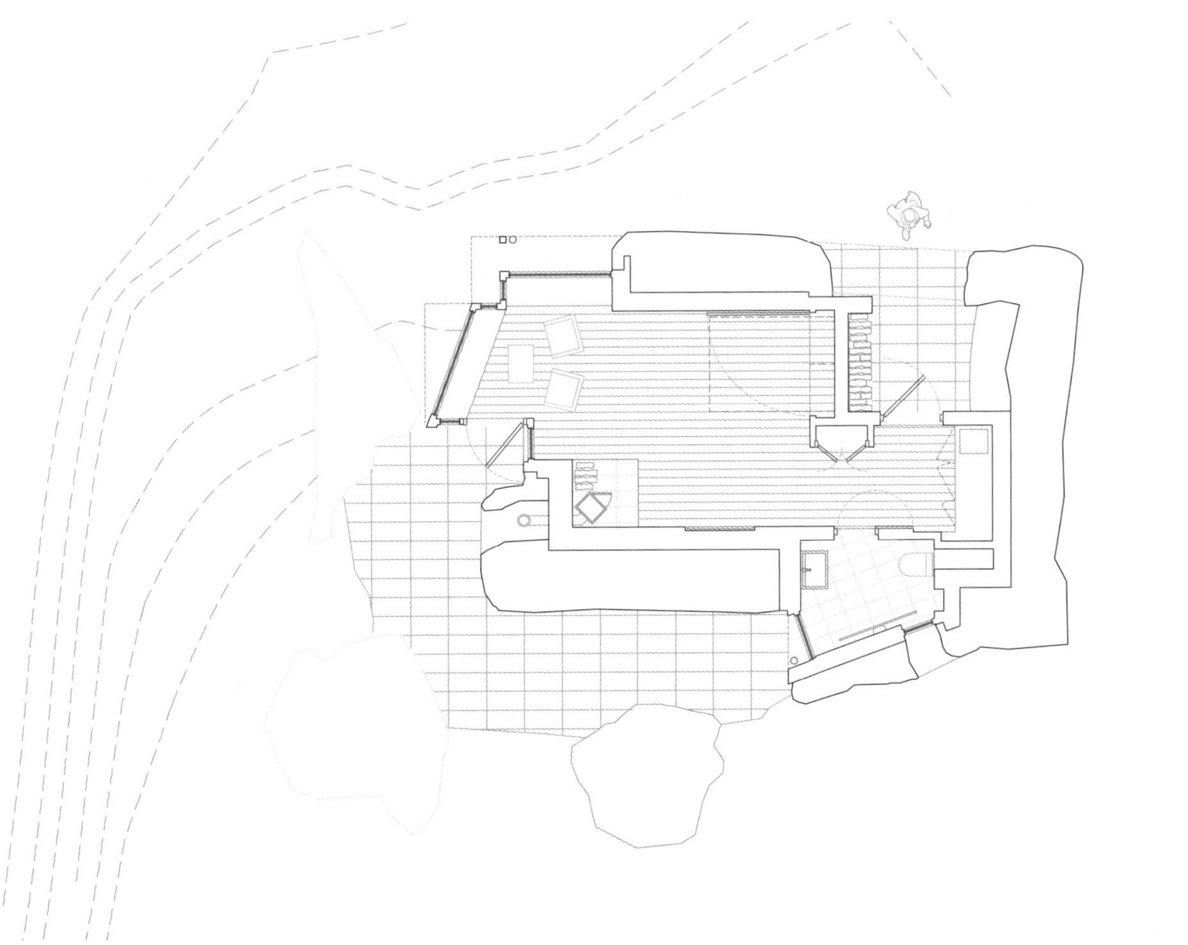

I

AV BEACH HOUSE JADRIJA

AV BEACH HOUSE JADRIJA

SIBENIK
CROATIA

CLIENT
Ante Vrban
AREA
70 m²
YEAR
2015
PHOTOGRAPHY
Architect Ante Vrban

AV Beach House Jadrija was designed as an architect's vacation home. This residence is an open, visually light house with glass façades that reflect the surrounding nature and sea, creating a chameleon effect. The idea was to offer enough privacy but still be very open to the sea, the beach and the pine trees in front of it. The pavilion is located in Jadrija, a popular seaside resort situated on an artificial peninsula at the entrance to St. Anthony Channel. Jadrija is a registered protected architectural site of the Croatian cultural heritage. The foundation of the house was built using recycled materials from an older building demolished on the site. The roof, which is sloped towards the backyard, is covered with a two-component polyurethane liquid membrane. This white color reflects sunlight and significantly reduces the internal temperature of the structure, making it resistant to extreme temperatures.

A South-west glass façade facing the sea
B Nighttime terrace view with pine trees

B

C

D

C Shaded areas provide space for relaxation
D Flowers offer a colorful contrast to the wooden terrace
E Existing pine trees have been incorporated into the terrace design
F Glass structure reflecting the surrounding nature

E

F

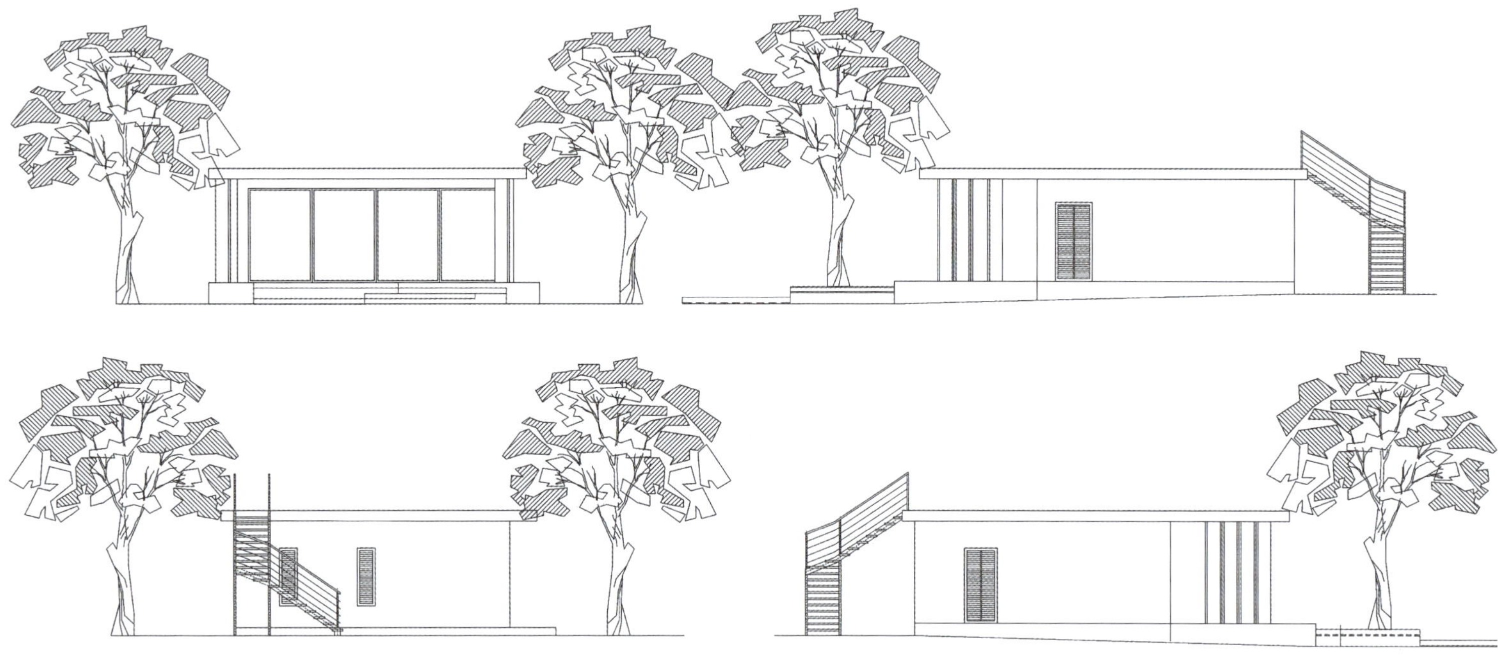

G

H

I

J

K

G Elevations
H Water-colored sketch of the project
I Terrace is split into different levels
J Living room with glass sliding doors
K Daytime terrace with pine trees

CANYAMEL

A

AREA
420 m²
YEAR
2021
PHOTOGRAPHY
Negre Studio

Canyamel is located on a site with breathtaking sea views on the north-east coast of Mallorca. The interior design took advantage of the site's context, creating setting that prioritizes the enjoyment of the views outside. By maintaining a clean and minimalist style, using simple lines and implementing materials such as natural stone, the impact of the surrounding nature was maximized. Natural light can be received from almost all angles of the house. Several outdoor seating areas are spread out over multiple levels, providing space for contemplation, relaxation and socializing. An expansive terrace with an infinity pool has been furnished with wicker chairs and loungers in a light color palette with deep blue accents that reference the ocean. Bordered only by glass fencing, these areas transition seamlessly to the surrounding water.

A Hammock chairs at window opening
B Outdoor seating overlooking the ocean

B

C Infinity pool view

C

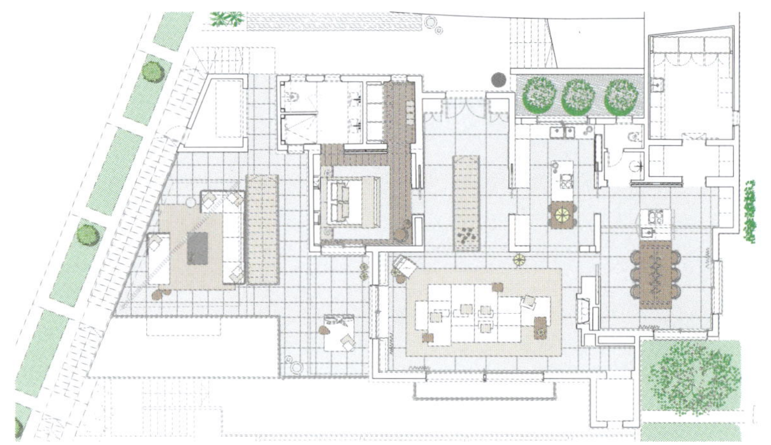

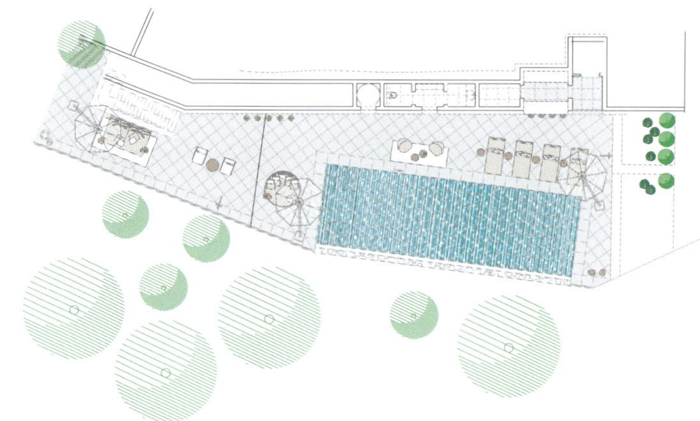

D E

F

D Main floor plan
E Terrace floor plan
F Terrace sea view
G Wicker armchairs backed by the ocean

KALIM BEACH HOUSE

A

KALIM BEACH HOUSE

PHUKET
THAILAND

OTHER CREATIVES
Lighting Studio Pum
AREA
700 m^2
YEAR
2019
PHOTOGRAPHY
Levi Wells (A, C, I, J, K)
Tawiporn
Thawornjaturawat (B, D)

The site of Kalim Beach House is on a hill with a 180-degree view of Kalim Bay. The house has four bedrooms, a large, shared living and dining area and a curved pool. Everything is contained within two large board-form concrete walls. The main focal point of the building is a vertical courtyard that keeps the surrounding spaces cool and ventilated. Given the spectacular bay views, the building faces west to take full advantage of the beautiful Andaman sunsets. To provide shade from the strong tropical sun and for added privacy, large sliding bamboo screens are installed in front of all upstairs bedrooms. Throughout the house, bamboo is used as a sunscreen, both vertically and horizontally. On the living level, a large infinity-edge pool stretches to the horizon, reflecting the sky and echoing the gentle curve of the bay.

A Exterior view with pool
B Ocean view

B

C

C Entrance area
D Kitchen
E Entrance area

D

E

F

G

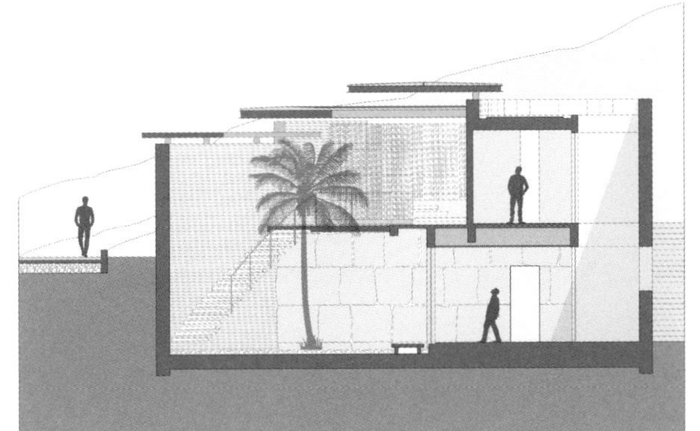

H I

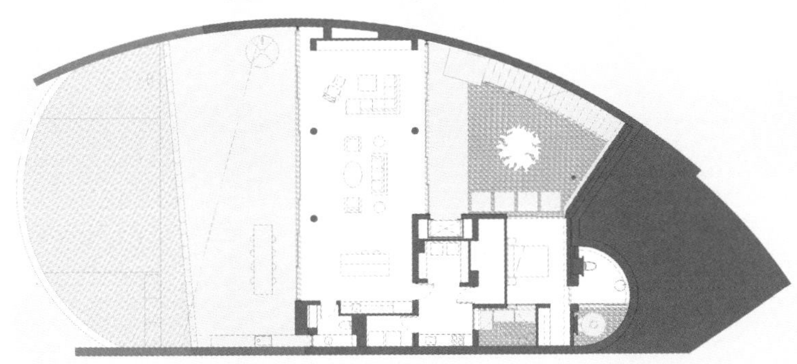

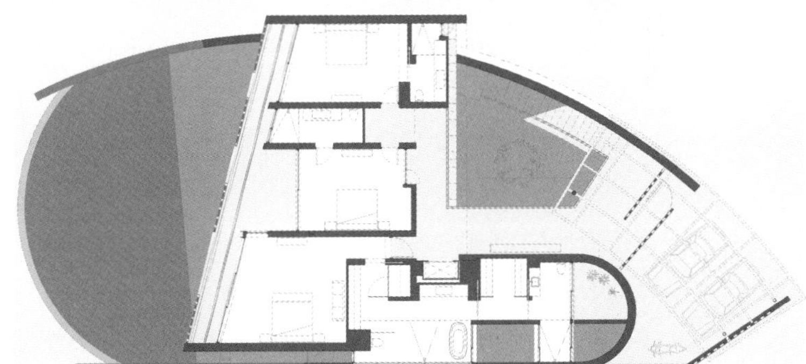

J K

F Bathroom
G Bamboo roof detail
H Section
I Section
J Ground floor plan
K First floor plan

HOUSE BY THE LAKE

A

HOUSE BY THE LAKE

LA CÔTE
SWITZERLAND

AREA
434 m²
YEAR
2019
PHOTOGRAPHY
Julien Lanoo
www.julienlanoo.com

Situated on the shores of Lake Geneva, this house in the canton of Vaud overlooks one of Switzerland's most unique sceneries. Through a contextual approach, the House by the Lake plays with the topography to become organically rooted. With its back to the north, hidden from its neighbors, the house privileges quiet views of the lake landscape. Local regulations required a pitched roof, a constraint the architects used to define the house's shelter with five gables instead of two. This, together with the fold in the main front, allows the family home to benefit from bespoke views throughout the day. On the façades, materials extend the organic expression of the house. With brick on the walls and clay tiles on the roof, the construction has earthy tones throughout. The use of untreated, oiled oak for the window frames reinforces these earthy tones for added warmth and connection to the landscape.

A Terrace facing the lake
B Bird's-eye view of House by the Lake

B

91

HOUSE BY THE LAKE

LA CÔTE
SWITZERLAND

C View of the south front

C

D

E

F

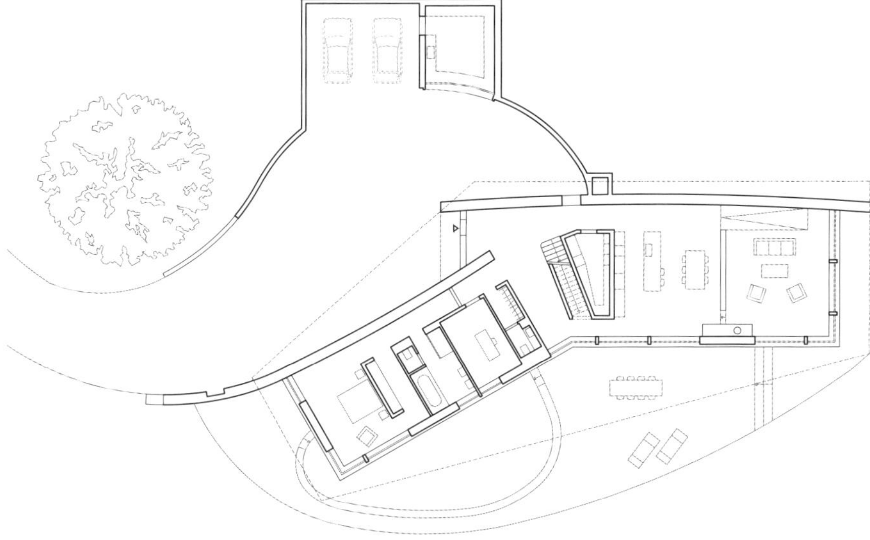

G

H

D Brick walls and clay tiles covering the roof
E Roof seen from the north end of the site
F Section
G Ground floor plan
H Site plan

LIDO BEACH HOUSE II

A

LIDO BEACH HOUSE II

LIDO BEACH
NY, USA

AREA
244 m²
YEAR
2021
PHOTOGRAPHY
Resolution: 4 Architecture

Situated on a flag lot at the corner of Lido Beach, this prefab house serves as a summer home for a writer and her family. The house seeks to establish a relationship with the surrounding dunes and beach, while at the same time referencing its cozy neighborhood. The private first floor includes a master suite, a second bedroom and bathroom. On the street side, windows are strategically placed to allow for ample daylight and natural ventilation while providing privacy. Along the west side of the home, the windows are more expansive, providing views of the dunes and beach. The second floor rises just above the dunes to take full advantage of the unobstructed views of the Atlantic Ocean. Full-height sliding glass doors open to two screened porches at the corners of the home, creating a seamless transition between inside and out.

A Front view
B Corner porch on the second floor

B

C

D

E F

C Corner porch with ocean view
D Outdoor shower
E Kitchen facing screened porch
F Roof deck

G

H

LIDO BEACH HOUSE II

LIDO BEACH
NY, USA

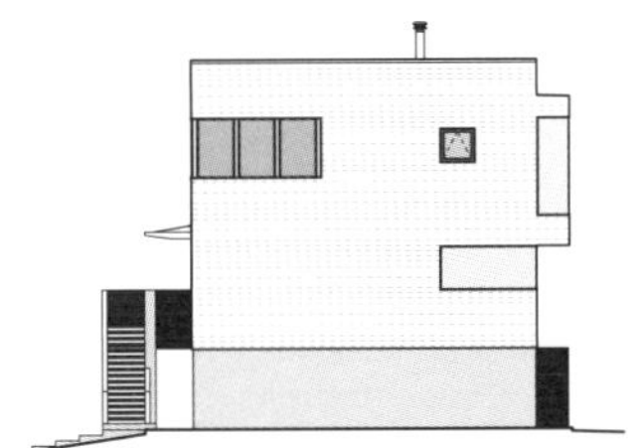
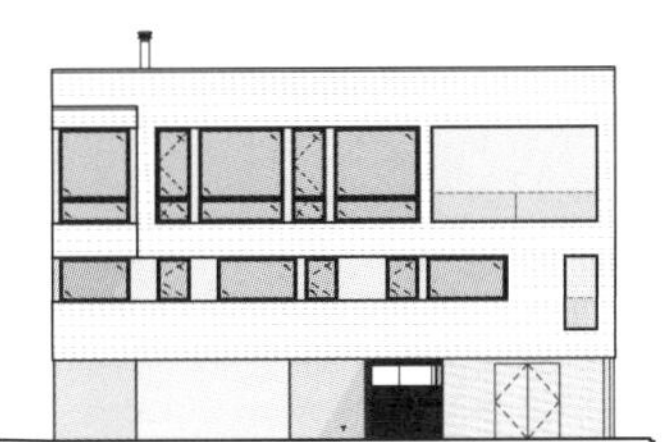

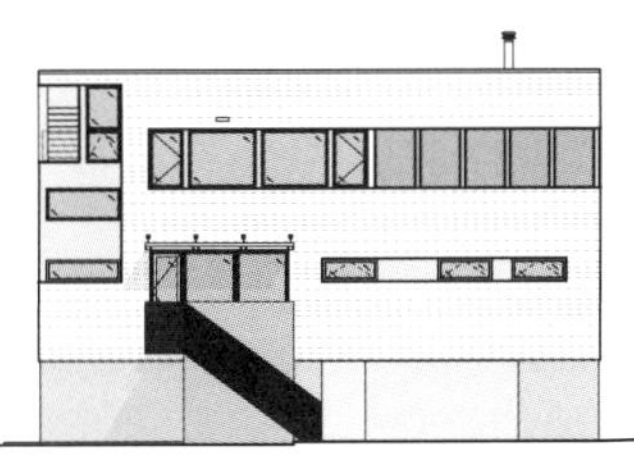

I J

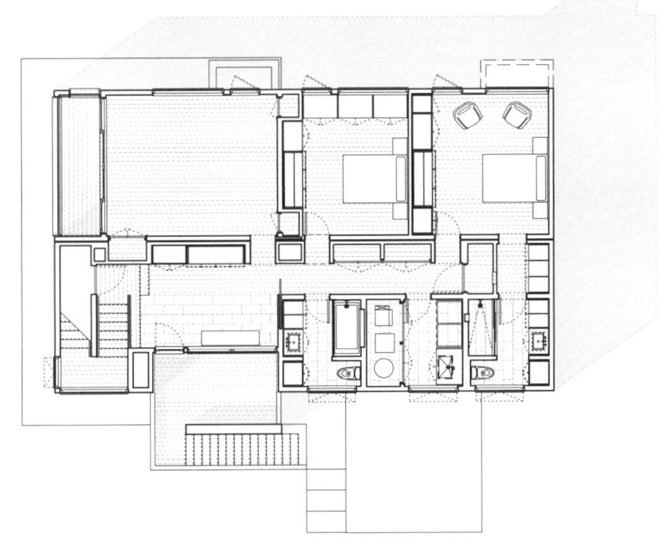
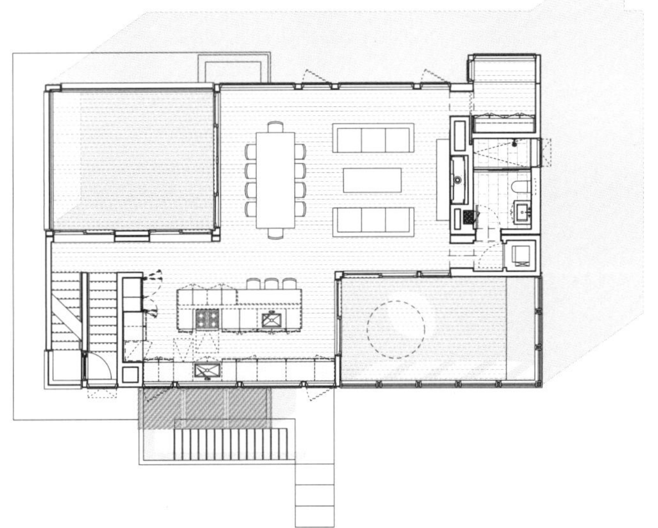

K L

G Kitchen
H Exterior view from beach
I North and west elevation
J South and east elevation
K First floor plan
L Second floor plan

DÜNENHAUS DIERHAGEN

A

DÜNENHAUS DIERHAGEN

DIERHAGEN
GERMANY

CLIENT
Kai Sternberg
Elke Werner
AREA
106 m^2
YEAR
2023
PHOTOGRAPHY
Kai Sternberg

The Dünenhaus Dierhagen, located on the Fischland peninsula, is situated in the immediate vicinity of the beach and leans directly against the dunes. The design features an asymmetrical gable, a black zinc roof, and black wooden windows set within a black larch wood façade. Despite its rough and modern exterior, the house exudes a warm and inviting atmosphere. The two-story entryway is flooded with natural light thanks to a skylight system and windows at the front and back. Sliding glass doors lead to the terraces, seamlessly connecting the inside and outside spaces and creating the sensation of being nestled within the seaside dunes. The interior features furniture and surfaces in oak and warm earth tones, accented by black accessories and lighting. On the upper floor, the loggia provides stunning views of the ocean. Additionally, large dormer windows offer a unique feature for the upper floor's bedroom and sauna.

A South-west façade
B Loggia sea view

B

C

C Kitchen
D Dining area
E Living area
F Two-story entrance area

D

E

F

G

H I

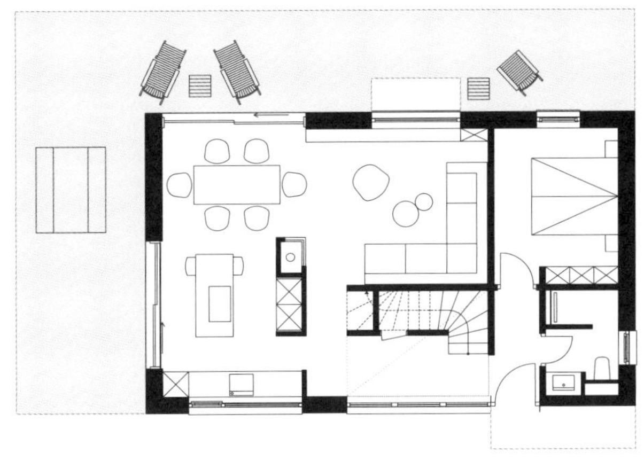

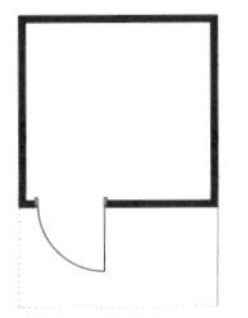

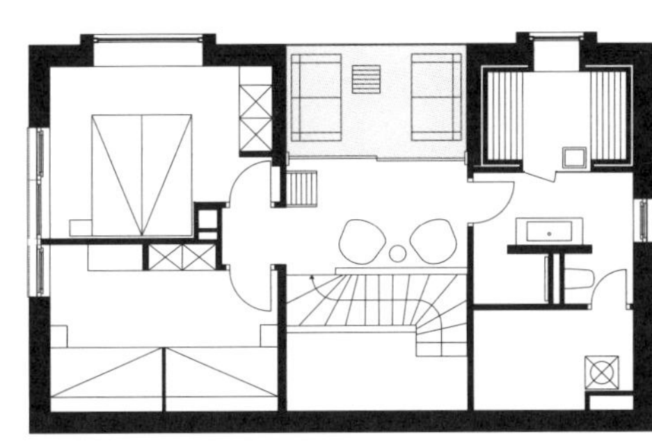

J K

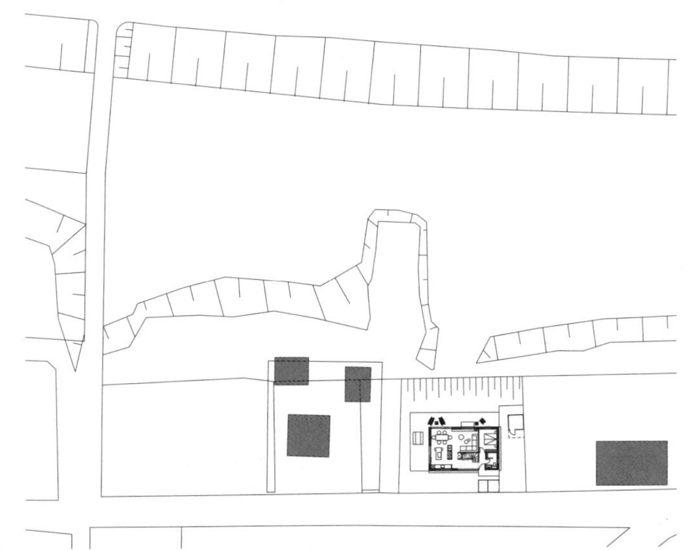

L

G Bedroom sea view
H Dormer window detail
I Larch wood façade
J Ground floor plan
K First floor plan
L Site plan

MASON

A

MASON

CHON BURI
THAILAND

LANDSCAPE DESIGN
RAFA
CLIENT
K Wave Company Limited
AREA
9,039 m^2
YEAR
2019
PHOTOGRAPHY
Ketsiree Wongwan (A)
Spaceshift Studio
www. spaceshiftstudio.com
(B, D, E, G, H)
Wara Suttiwan (C, F)

Located on Na Jomtien Beach in Chon Buri, the Mason Pool Villa Resort sits on a beachfront terrain as high as a four-story building. The resort's design incorporates green roofs and natural textures such as concrete, wood, and stone to harmonize with the surrounding environment of sand, sea, and tropical flora. Due to the steep site and limited beach access, the common area walking paths were designed to offer an immersive experience for users, simulating the texture and feel of a rock cave. The pool villas are categorized into four distinct room types, namely the garden pool villa, duplex grand pool villa, beachside seaview pool villa, and beachfront grand pool villa. The villas are arranged in a descending order, allowing for an unobstructed view of the ocean. To access the villas, visitors must stroll along the lush rooftops, which blend into the verdant tropical surroundings.

A Beachfront grand pool villa
B Aerial view of the site

B

C

D

C Common area and villas with green roofing overlooking the sea
D Lobby and stairway to the beach
E Duplex villa with elevated bathroom and pool access

E

F

G H

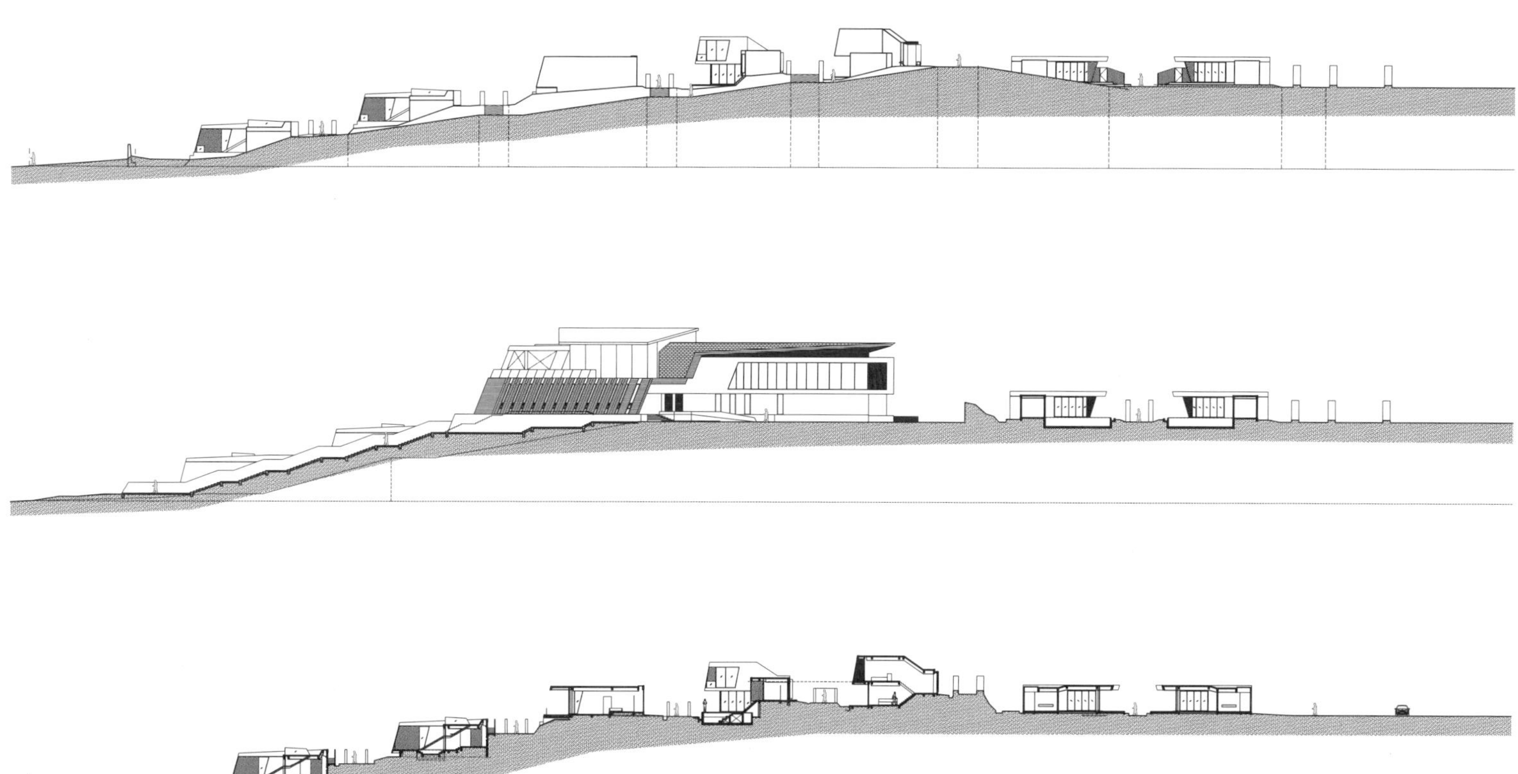

I

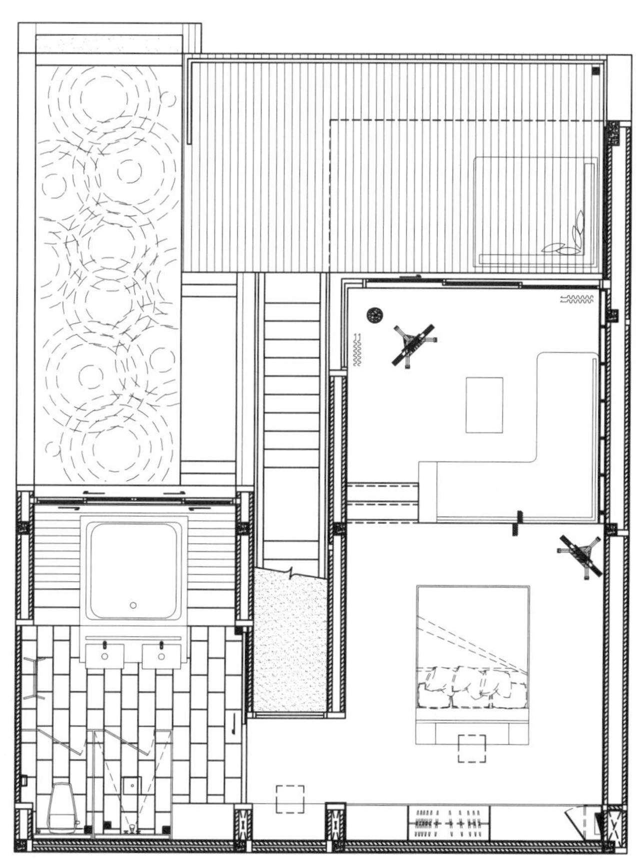

J

F Beachfront pool villa terrace
G Bedroom sea view
H Bathroom with carved opening providing natural light
I Elevations
J Beachfront grand pool villa floor plan

SEA RANCH ESCAPE

A

SEA RANCH ESCAPE

THE SEA RANCH
CA, USA

INTERIOR DESIGN
Leverone Design
LANDSCAPE DESIGN
Gualala Nursery & Trading
AREA
362 m²
YEAR
2015
PHOTOGRAPHY
Joe Fletcher
www.joefletcher.com

Tucked in between tufts of cypress trees on a jagged cliff overlooking the Pacific Ocean, an architectural assembly becomes a family vacation home. Located in the 1960s planned community of Sea Ranch, the home shares common elements with its neighbors – muted colors, vertical wood siding, dramatic views – while incorporating design elements of its own. The house harmoniously blends light and dark, soft and hard elements, seamlessly connecting the interior and exterior environments. The exterior design features clear cedar siding complemented by black-framed windows, while the interior showcases an interplay of soft wood components, floor-to-ceiling windows, and dark flooring. Living spaces are horizontally oriented to the ocean, with a sloped ceiling and aligned furniture drawing the eye to an expansive line of windows. Bedroom and office offer vertical openings for contemplation.

A Window seat overlooking the Pacific
B South façade and guest house nestled into the surrounding nature

B

C Staircase
D Living area ocean view
E Kitchen framed in vertical timber structures

C

D

F

G H

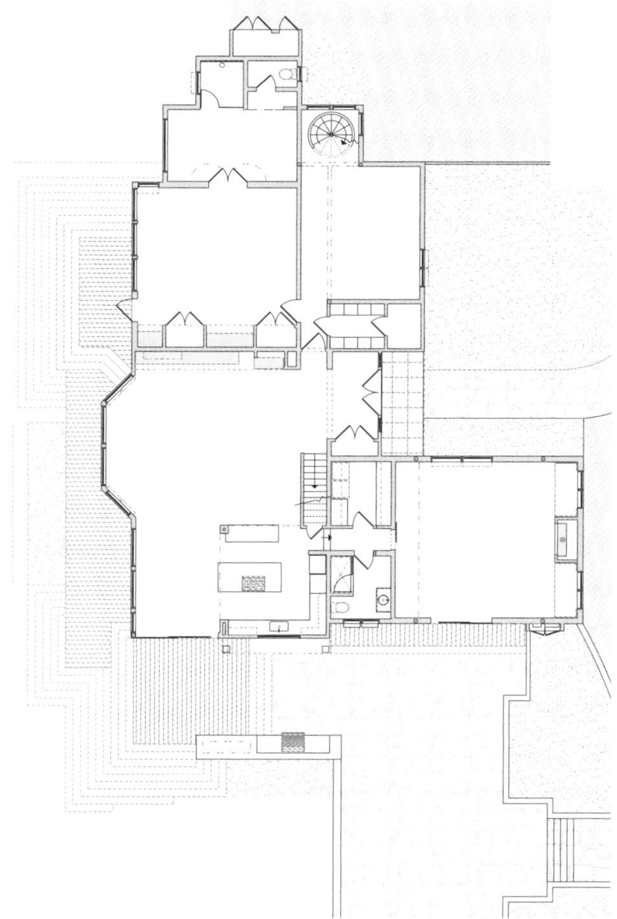

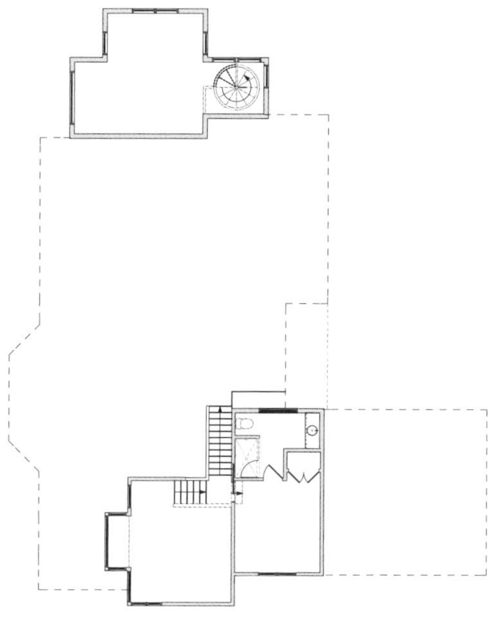

I J

F Master bathroom with oversized architectural tub and ocean views
G Master bathroom detail
H First floor office ocean view
I Ground floor plan
J First floor plan

BUCKLETON'S BOAT SHED

A

BUCKLETON'S BOAT SHED

TĀWHARANUI PENINSULA
NEW ZEALAND

AREA
170 m^2
YEAR
2020
PHOTOGRAPHY
Patrick Reynolds

Buckleton's Boat Shed is an experimental house project that engages in the act of building on the vulnerable coastline of New Zealand in this climate uncertain world. The overall composition is bold but simple and reminiscent of a boat or ark floating above the land. It sits on piles that extend 12 meters into the ground to resist coastal erosion from storm inundation, sea-level rise or overland flow. Nature can alter the coastal environment below the house while occupation can continue for generations to come. As is typical of the coastline of New Zealand, land is often contained by the native bush and then opens to the expanse of the ocean. The concept sought a form that was generated by the site constraints and opportunities for occupation; lifting off the ground for flooding, gently rising to the wide elevated view over the beach, touching the land lightly toward the road to receive a boat and controlling privacy from the public reserve and neighbors.

A Entry to the house
B House viewed from the beach
C Upstairs corridor

B C

D

E

D View to the beach from living room
E View from beach
F Kitchen
G Living room area

F

G

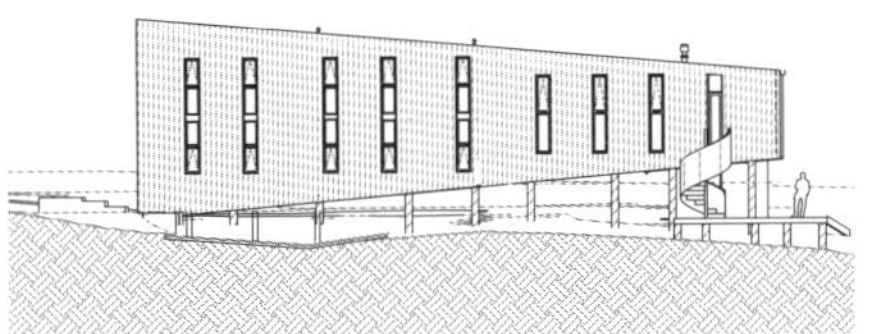

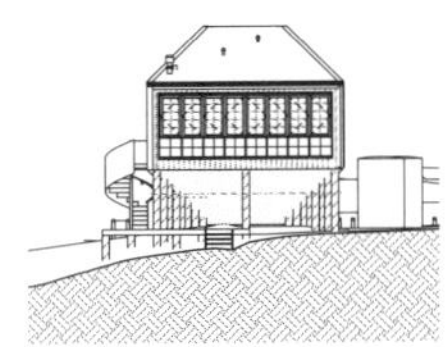

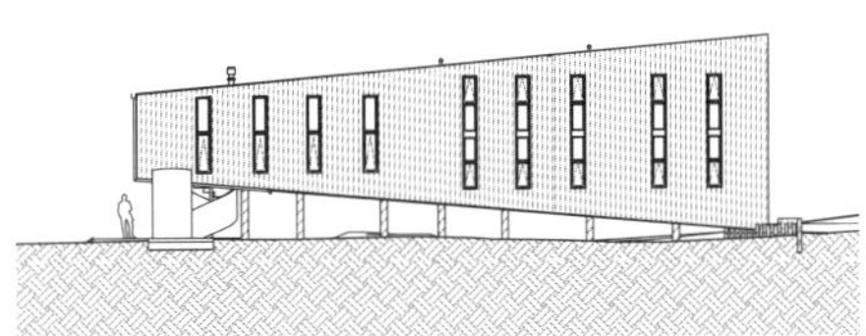

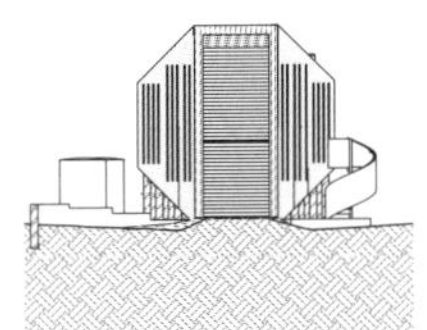

I

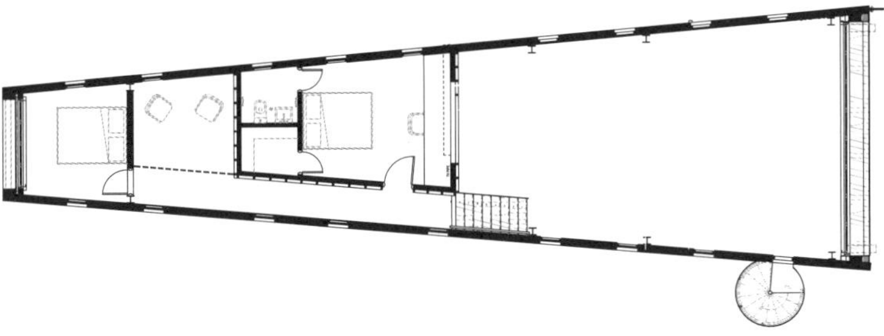

J

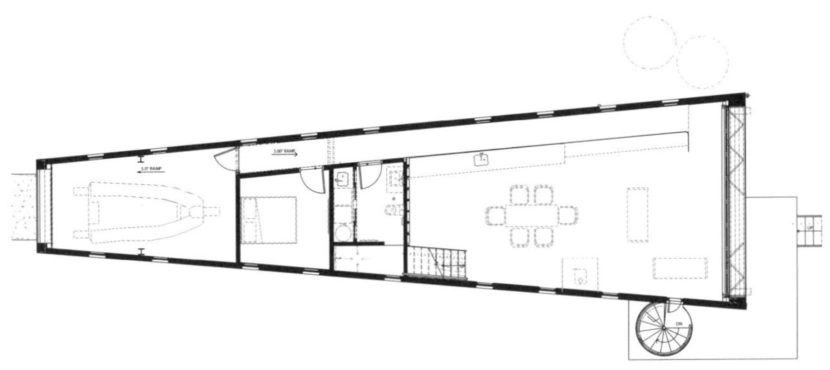

K

H Sheltered deck space under the house
I Longitudinal and cross elevation
J First floor plan
K Ground floor plan

SANTO BY THE SEA

A

125

SANTO BY THE SEA

VAN PHONG BAY
VIETNAM

CLIENT
Phan Nhu Thao
AREA
850 m^2
YEAR
2022
PHOTOGRAPHY
Hiroyuki Oki

The inspiration behind the creation of this residence was the owner's desire to infuse Mediterranean revival with architectural elements. The vision for Santo by the Sea was to feature grand arched doorways that not only embrace the beautiful surrounding nature but also flood the interior with natural light. As a symbolic nod to its origins, the house is adorned with raw plaster both inside and outside; the exposed cement ceiling serves as a canvas that highlights the azure ocean and the blue sky. The house's interior layout is thoughtfully divided into the main ground floor for the owner and an upper floor dedicated to guests. A staircase positioned outside serves as a connecting path between the two levels. At the heart of the residence, an expansive pool area forms a tranquil bridge between these distinct spaces.

A Arched windows facing the sea
B Aerial view of the residence

B

C

C Yellow accents in the interior
D Arched windows offer sea views
E Front view of the house

D

E

F

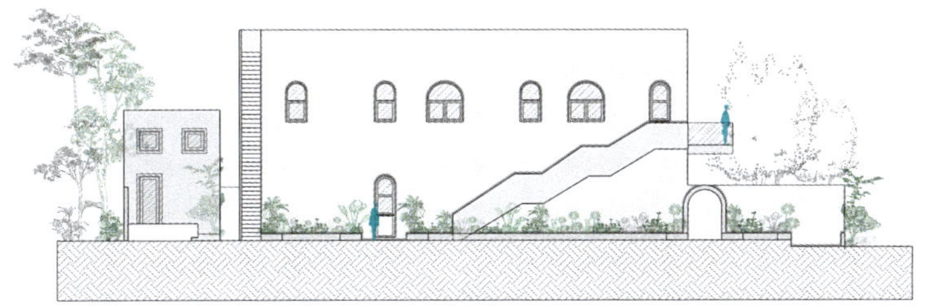

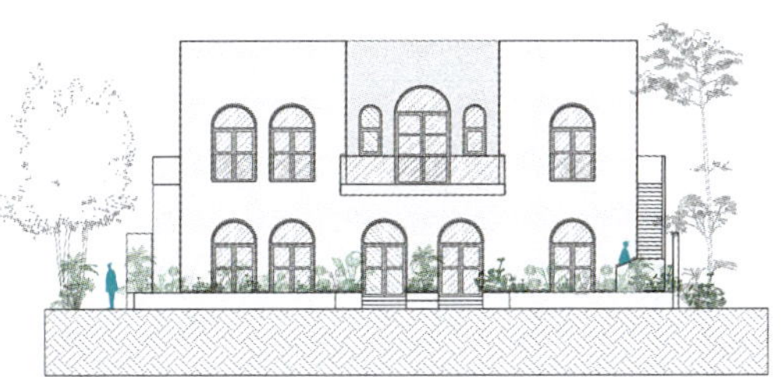

G

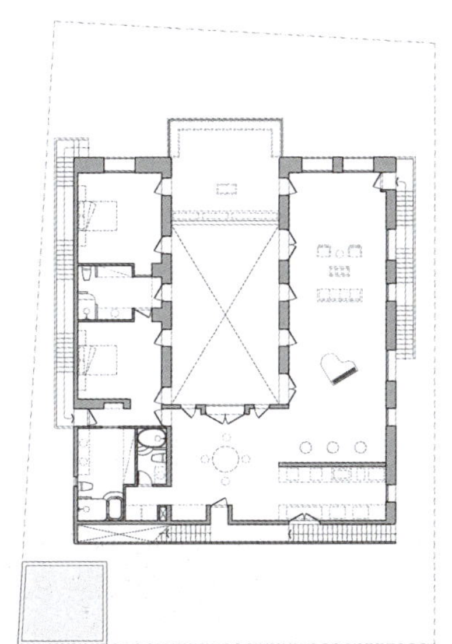

H

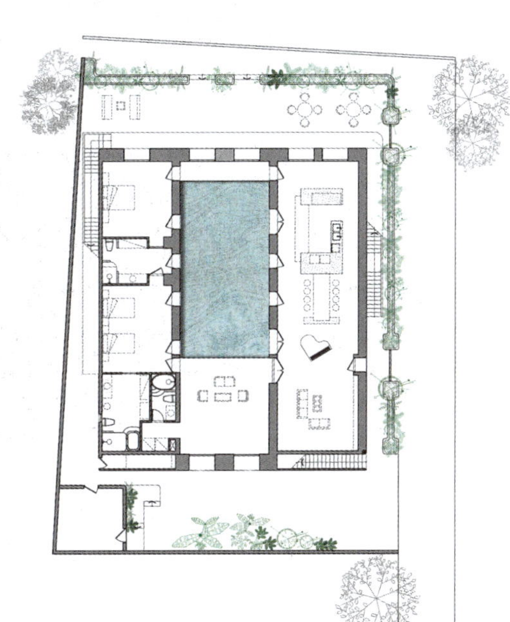

I

F Walkway leading over the pool area
G Side and front elevation
H First floor plan
I Ground floor plan

FULFORD HOUSE

A

131

FULFORD HOUSE

AUCKLAND
NEW ZEALAND

LANDSCAPE DESIGN
John Helyar
CLIENT
Victoria & Dean Fulford
AREA
487 m^2
YEAR
2021
PHOTOGRAPHY
Simon Wilson
www.simonwilson.co.nz

Fulford House is located on the edge of the Hauraki Gulf. The site's steep contour provided the opportunity to create a large three level home, with the basement cut into the slope, allowing the pool to have an infinity edge view of the harbor. The home was designed for a close-knit family who wanted a space that evokes relaxed living, but also provides activities and spaces to share. The entrance to the home is on the ground floor, which is on the mid-level, so the home reads as only two levels. The basement opens out to the large pool and can be accessed by internal stairs and the external spiral staircase. The mid-level living area has a large, covered patio that mirrors the interior layout with a cooking area, dining area and lounge area. The large sliding doors can be moved in either direction. The four bedrooms on the top level each have access to the outside deck, allowing for expansive water views.

A Entry view showing the upper two levels
B Top floor deck with firepit, accessed via the bedroom

B

C Mid-level outdoor patio with dining area facing Hauraki Gulf

C

D

E

F

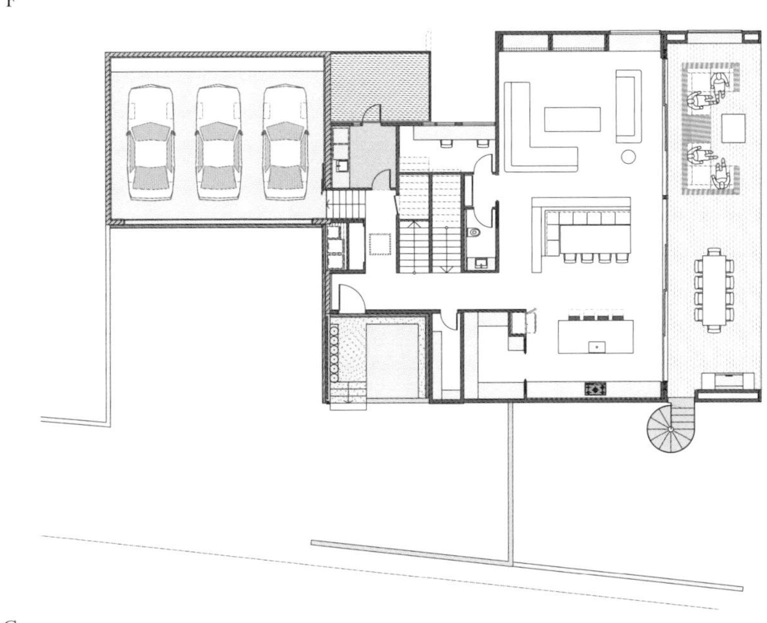

G

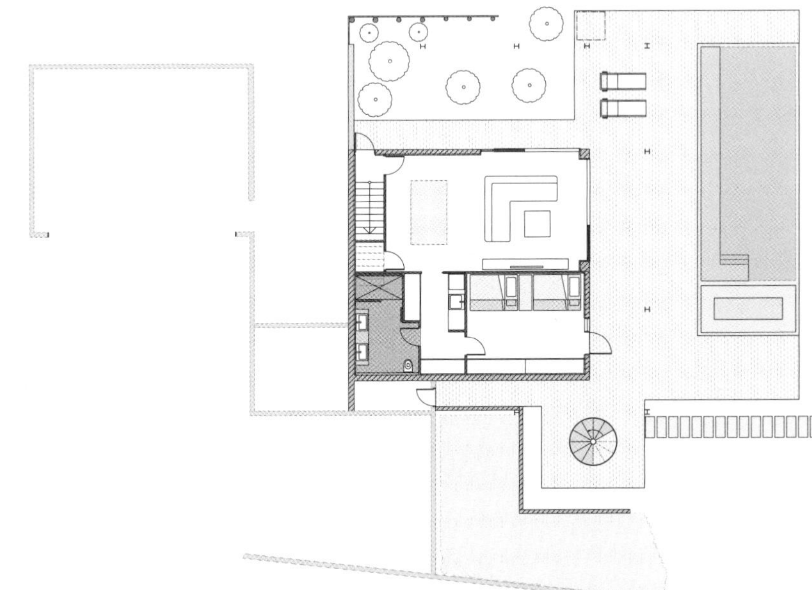

H

D Basement floor infinity pool view
E Aerial view of outdoor spaces and landscaping
F First floor plan
G Ground floor plan
H Basement floor plan

CASA SANTA TERESA

A

CASA SANTA TERESA

AJACCIO
FRANCE

AREA
400 m²
YEAR
2020
PHOTOGRAPHY
Thibaut Dini
www.thibautdini.co

Casa Santa Teresa is a recreation of a 1950's beach house located on a site offering expansive views of the Gulf of Ajaccio in Corsica. The holiday residence aims to retain the character of the older building, while some of the interior walls have been removed to create spacious living areas with unobstructed sea views. It was crucial for the design to adapt to the environment of nature, light and relief. Built on a slope, the four-story house consists of cascading levels, three of which provide access to outdoor spaces such as decks and terraces facing the sea. A smooth white façade and raw materials such as reclaimed brick, chestnut wood, natural stone and glazed terracotta tiles pay hommage to the Mediterranean. Indoor and outdoor spaces are balanced by the use of stripped shutters and pivoting doors. Plants and trees frame the natural stone terraces and pathways that lead to the beach.

A First-floor-deck dining area with sea view
B First floor deck and ground floor terrace
C Top-down view of the residence

B C

D

E

D Living and dining area
E Dining area detail
F Living area sea view
G Master bedroom sea view

F

G

H

I J

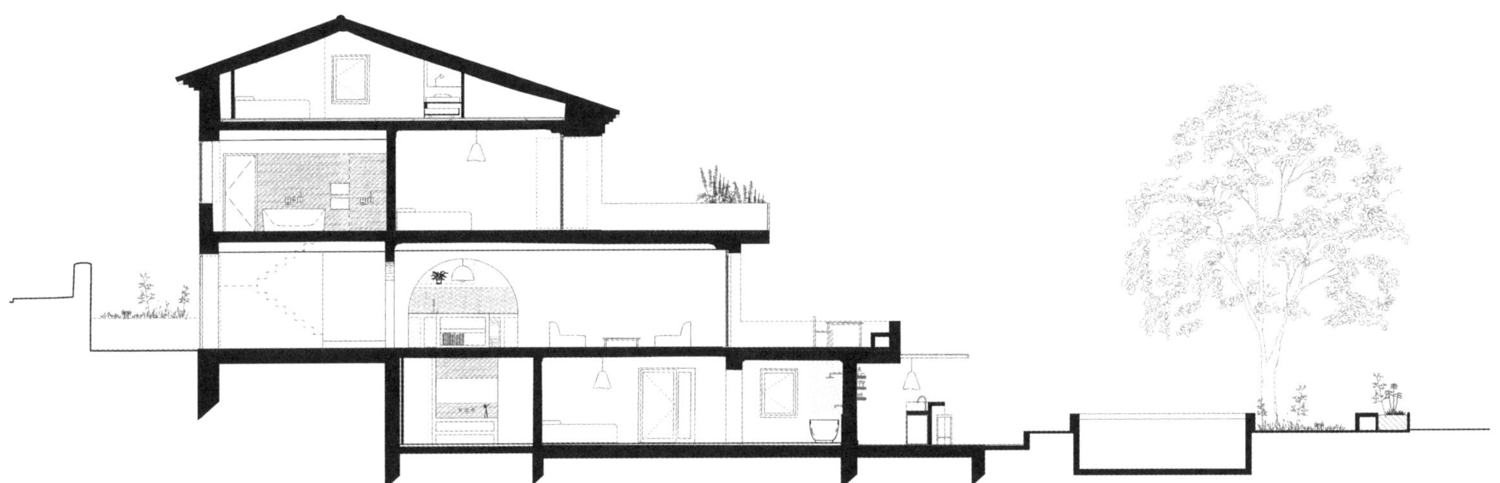

K

H Terrace and pool
I Pathway framed by greenery
J Terraces split into different levels
K Section

TRANSFORMATION HOUSE WI.

A

TRANSFORMATION HOUSE WI.

ASCONA
SWITZERLAND

AREA
125 m²
YEAR
2022
PHOTOGRAPHY
Hannes Henz
www.hanneshenz.ch

The stunning rock topography of the steep slope features as the supporting element of the project. The existing natural stone retaining walls, which seem to grow organically out of the rock, are incorporated into the project. In order to best integrate the new architecture into the rock, the project also includes natural stone walls. The house opens to the mountain with an all-glass façade, allowing the rock to be tangibly integrated into the interior and creating a pleasant reflective light. A stone filter façade on the valley side, which serves as a conceptual sun protection to prevent the glass façade behind it from heating up excessively, evokes the atmosphere of a ruin. The interior and exterior flow seamlessly into each other; the house, the outdoor loggia and the swimming pool form a visual unit. The roof provides an additional, easily accessible outdoor space and storage area.

A Exterior view of the swimming pool
B Exterior view of the building

B

C

D

E

C Living room
D Dining space
E Bedroom

F G

H

F Basement floor plan
G Ground floor plan
H Elevation with mountain
I Exterior detail

I

CASA PUJOL-OTAEGUI

A

CASA PUJOL-OTAEGUI

MATANZAS
CHILE

AREA
239.7 m²
YEAR
2021
PHOTOGRAPHY
Nico Saieh
www.nicosaieh.cl

The house is located in the northern zone of Matanzas, at the top of a slight slope, which leads to a 65-meter cliff that ends at the beach. The general design is influenced by three main factors: to protect an exterior sector from the strong winds that prevail in the area, to maintain privacy from the neighbors, and to take full advantage of the sea views. Therefore, a U-shaped volume was built. Two parallel volumes face the neighboring boundaries, the third is totally permeable and parallel to the coastal edge. As a result, there is an outdoor patio in the middle, protected from the wind. The common areas are the central axis of the house, while the rest of the programmatic elements are distributed in the two volumes perpendicular to it. Semi-open courtyards provide better lighting. The main structure of the house is made up of metal frames, the secondary structure is made up of impregnated pine.

A Aerial view
B Outdoor patio east façade

B

C

D

E

C External view
D Outdoor patio east façade
E Aerial view

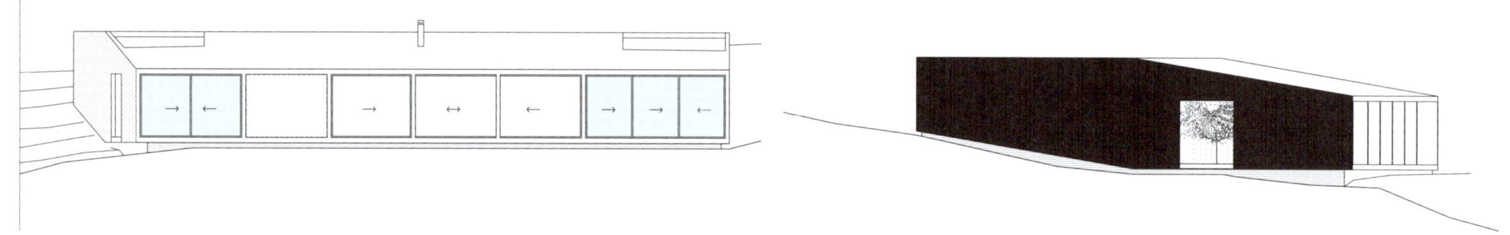

F G

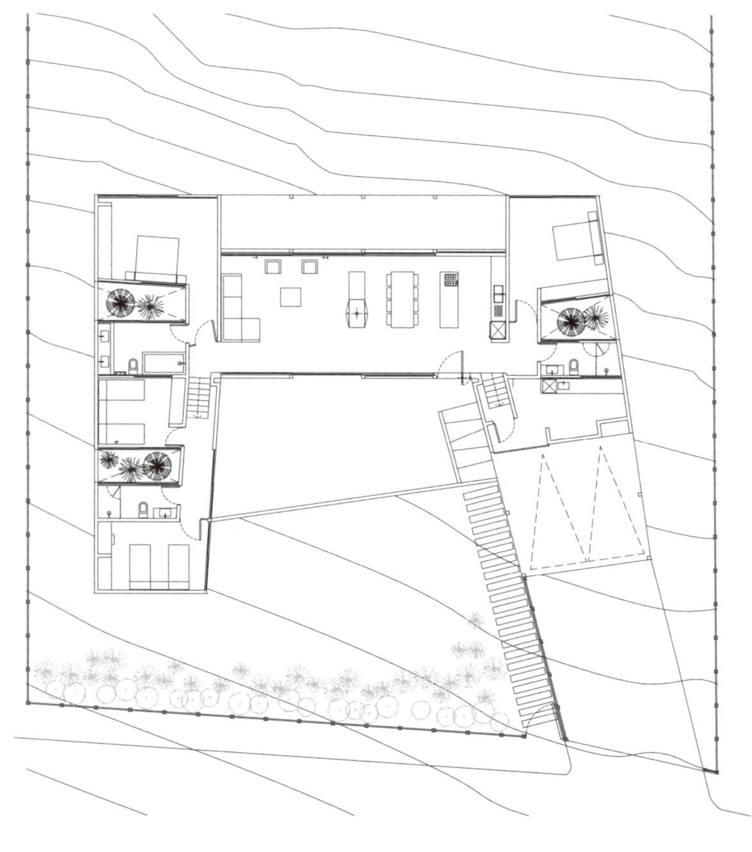

H

F West elevation
G North elevation
H Ground floor plan
I West façade
J Detail of north façade

I

J

LAGOON HOUSE

A

LAGOON HOUSE

STINSON BEACH
CA, USA

INTERIOR DESIGN
Monica Cardanini Interior Design
LANDSCAPE DESIGN
Boxleaf Design
AREA
269 m^2
YEAR
2018
PHOTOGRAPHY
Joe Fletcher
www.joefletcher.com

An unusual two-lot property in Stinson Beach is the site of a dramatic horizontal architectural composition that is subtle from the street but opens into view-filled pavilions toward the lagoon and coastline. In the living room, a large poured concrete fireplace is flanked by tall corner windows that draw the eye across the lagoon to the dramatic ridges of the coastal range. A massive opening to the outdoors allows the residents to move seamlessly between the living room and the outdoor patio. The home features a variety of construction materials, which create an interplay of soft wood structures and black metal elements. Cedar siding is used both horizontally and vertically, a blackened steel C-channel serves as an overhead track for the front door, oversized dark aluminum-framed windows provide natural light, and Douglas fir beams accent the living room pavilion.

A Living room opening to outdoor patio
B Living room lagoon view

B

C North façade facing the lagoon

D

E F

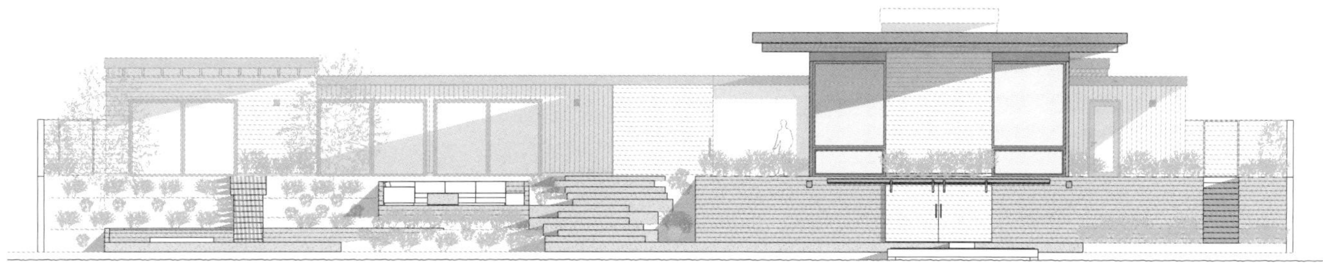

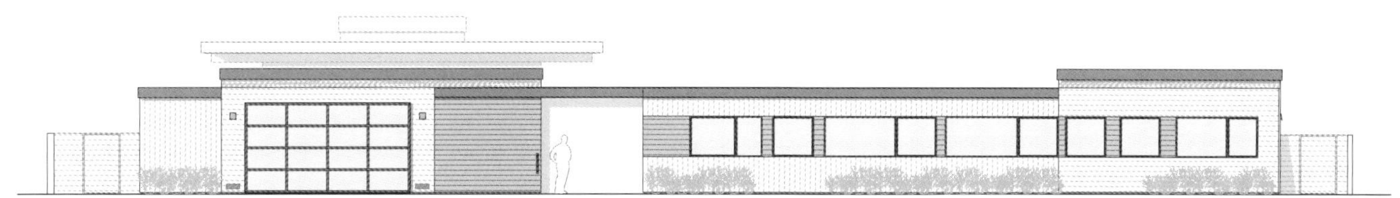

G

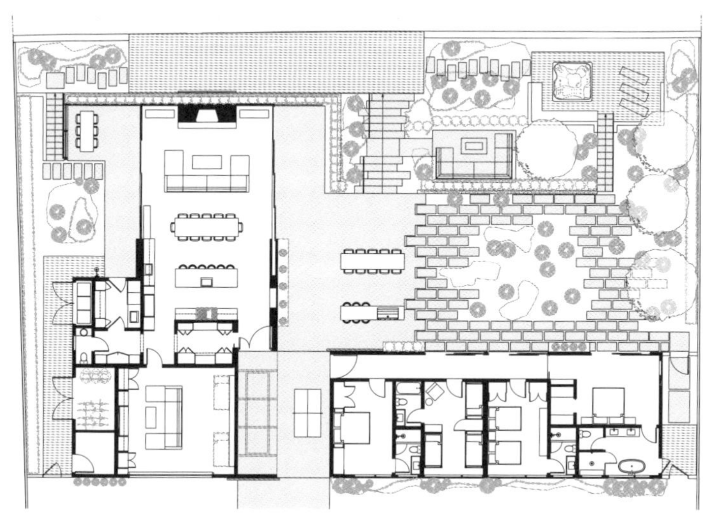

H

D Breezeway doubling as lounge and game area
E Hallway with cedar ceiling
F Kitchen with island counter
G Elevations
H Floor plan

STRANDHOUSE

A

161

STRANDHOUSE

HERMOSA BEACH
CA, USA

INTERIOR DESIGN
Jorie Clark Design
AREA
320 m²
YEAR
2020
PHOTOGRAPHY
Art Gray Photography
www. artgrayphoto.com

Located just south of the pier in Hermosa Beach, Strandhouse aims to be a model for the beach house typology and shotgun lot that is common throughout coastal Southern California. Volumetrically, the house is expressed as a simple rectangle, conceived as a framing device, focusing one's attention to the beach, the ocean and the sky, while calming the surrounding visual noise. The house is divided into three levels, each with a unique vantage point and distinct relationship to The Strand. The ground floor is conceived as an extension of the beach and its attention is absorbed by the activity before it. The main living space occupies the first floor, perched above The Strand its focus is on the ocean. Completely detached from the beach, the second floor focuses upward to the calm of the horizon and sky. A central stair core connects all levels, along with a pair of large, frosted windows.

A Second floor bedroom ocean view with focus on the sky
B First floor living room ocean view

B

C

D

C Living and kitchen space
D Kitchen detail
E Ground floor family room with access to the beach
F Balcony ocean view

STRANDHOUSE

HERMOSA BEACH
CA, USA

E

F

G

G Sunset beach façade
H Ground floor plan
I First floor plan
J Second floor plan

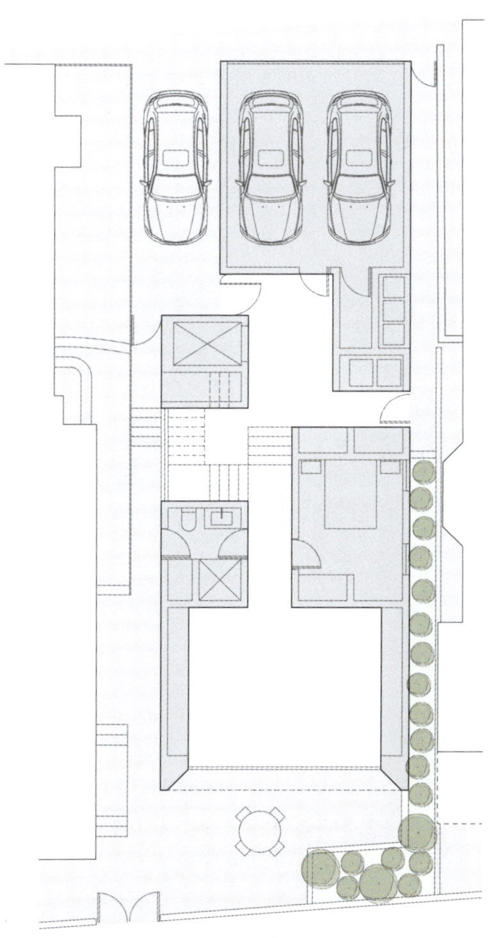

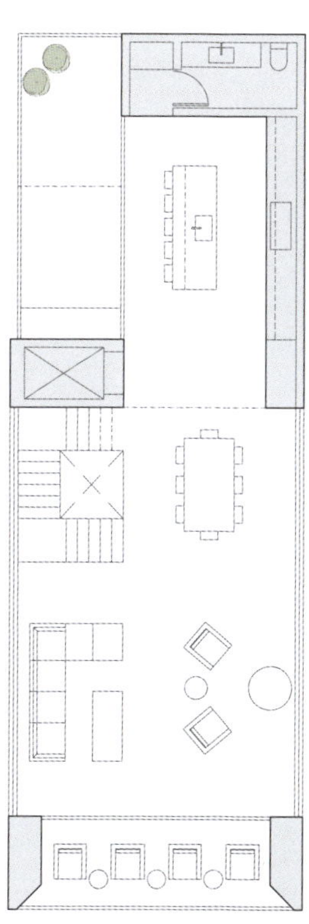

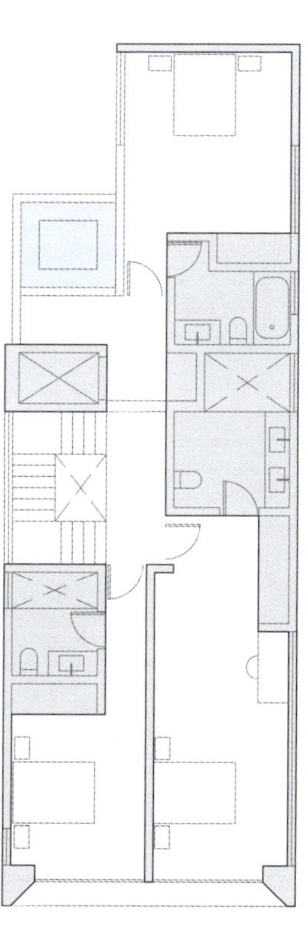

H I J

CLIFF FRONT 7

CARBON HOUSE

CLIFF FRONT 7 – CARBON HOUSE

INTERIOR DESIGN
Alexis Dornier, Tim Russo
AREA
275 m²
YEAR
2019
PHOTOGRAPHY
Kie
www.kiearch.com

This tropical modern villa in South Kuta maintains a consistent palette of over 100-year-old teak from Java, reclaimed ironwood from Kalimantan, andesite, terrazzo, local limestone, and floor-to-ceiling windows. The dominant gesture of the house is its polygonal shading element, which introduces a semi-covered transitional space that connects the interior to the exterior. Various folds in the roof provide a sense of protection and privacy. Each of the four bedrooms bears its own signature as a result of the project's overarching architectural narrative. The ceiling, clad in reclaimed teak, provides a stark contrast to the limestone walls, which continue the geometric theme on a different scale. The individually cut stone slabs were sourced from a local quarry. An expansive garden landscape cascades from the angular infinity pool, backed by the Indian Ocean.

A Living and dining space opening toward the polygonal roof element
B West façade facing the Indian Ocean

B

C Roof detail
D Roof structure connecting the interior and exterior of the house
E Bedrooms are accessed from the porch

C

D

F

G H

I

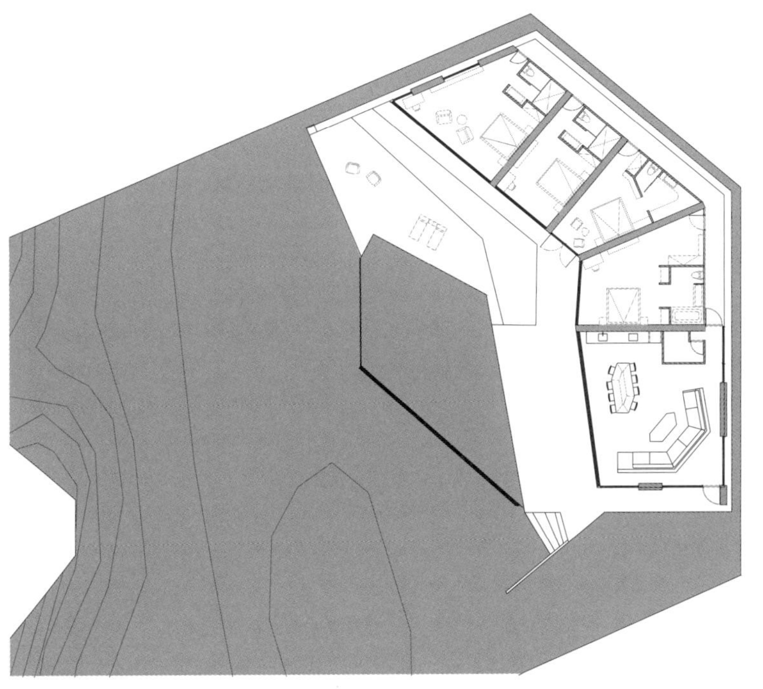

J

F Bedroom
G Porch backed by the ocean
H Bathtub in opened up bathroom
I West elevation
J Floor plan

CURRUMBIN BEACHFRONT RESIDENCE

A

CURRUMBIN BEACHFRONT RESIDENCE

CURRUMBIN
AUSTRALIA

CLIENT
RSL Art Union Qld
AREA
309 m^2
YEAR
2022
PHOTOGRAPHY
Kristian van der Beek
www.kristianbeek.com

The Currumbin Beachfront Residence is idyllically set on the coastline of Currumbin Beach in Gold Coast, Australia. This coastal three-story oasis was commissioned as a prize home and designed to take advantage of its unique location with direct beachfront access. The three key features of the site are the view, the abundance of natural light and the exposure to prevailing coastal breezes. Thus, the form of the building fans out towards the ocean with the primary spaces being pushed toward this part of the site. The secondary spaces are then sheltered behind for a more private experience. The connection to the landscape is promoted through the residences' courtyard spaces and a series of outdoor entertaining areas. The residence's materiality also reflects the coastal temperament through the use of low-maintenance natural elements that are well-suited to seaside conditions.

A Exterior and interior view
B Master bedroom
C Southern view

B C

D

E F

G

D Exterior view
E Bathroom
F First floor living room
G Dining area

H

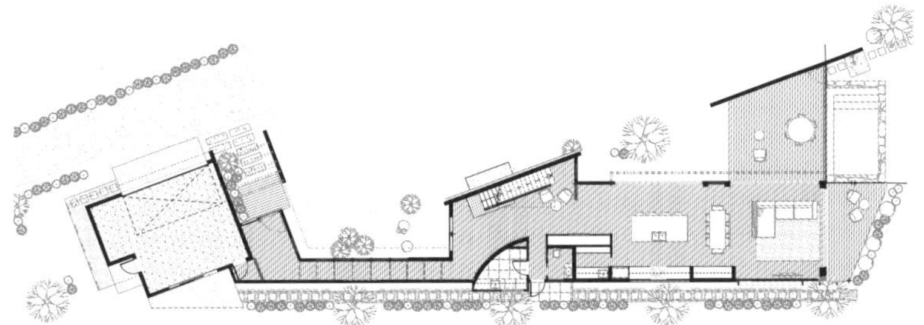

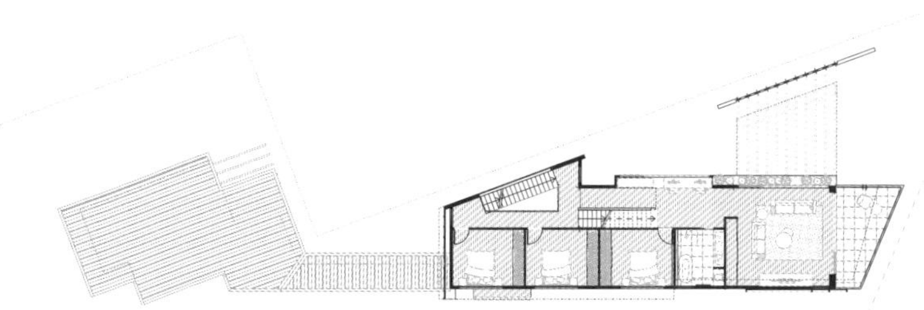

I J

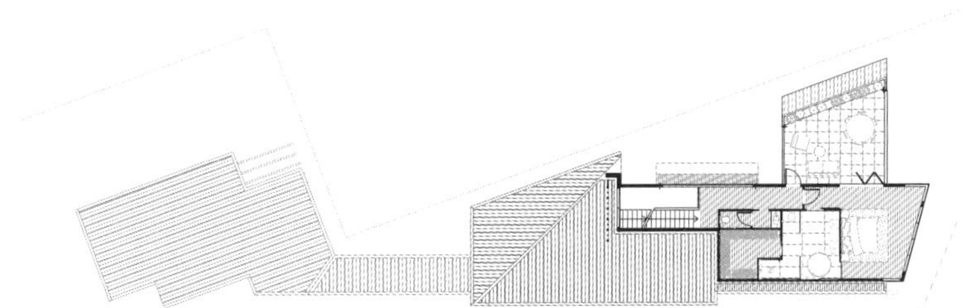

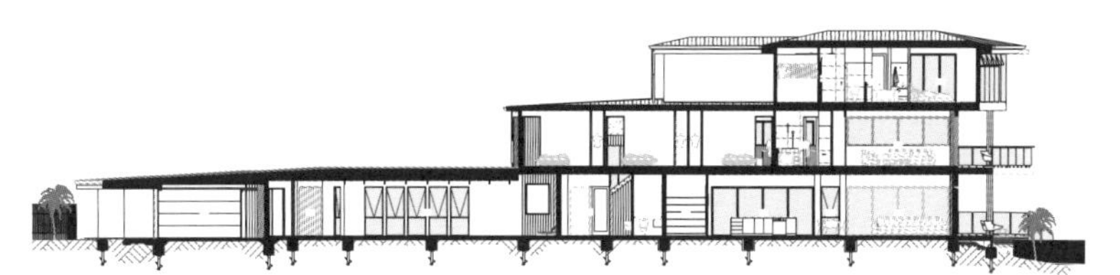

K L

H Exterior deck
I Ground floor plan
J First floor plan
K Second floor plan
L Section

HOUSE G

A

HOUSE G

SCHONDORF AM AMMERSEE
GERMANY

AREA
155 m²
YEAR
2019
PHOTOGRAPHY
Caro Dentler
www.permat-design.de

The house is situated on a subtle incline on a narrow site by Lake Ammersee in Bavaria. By incorporating a retaining wall featuring trough planters, steps, and seating, the sloped terrain has been transformed into a charming outdoor area. The building is constructed entirely of timber, except for the parts that touch the ground. The design of the house is inspired by the boats and fisherman's homes commonly found in the region, with the terrace hovering above the garden like a pier. Special attention was paid to utilizing sustainable and environmentally friendly materials while minimizing the use of adhesives and sealants. Solid planks of silver fir were joined together mechanically with dovetail joints to create a wood panel that is free from glue and pollutants. The sleek silver fir interior, paired with white-pigmented oiling on the surfaces, brightens the space and adds a touch of refinement.

A One-story gable façade
B Plant-filled stair detail
C Living area lake view

B C

D

E

D Guest area kitchen
E Ground floor hallway
F Main kitchen

F

G

H I

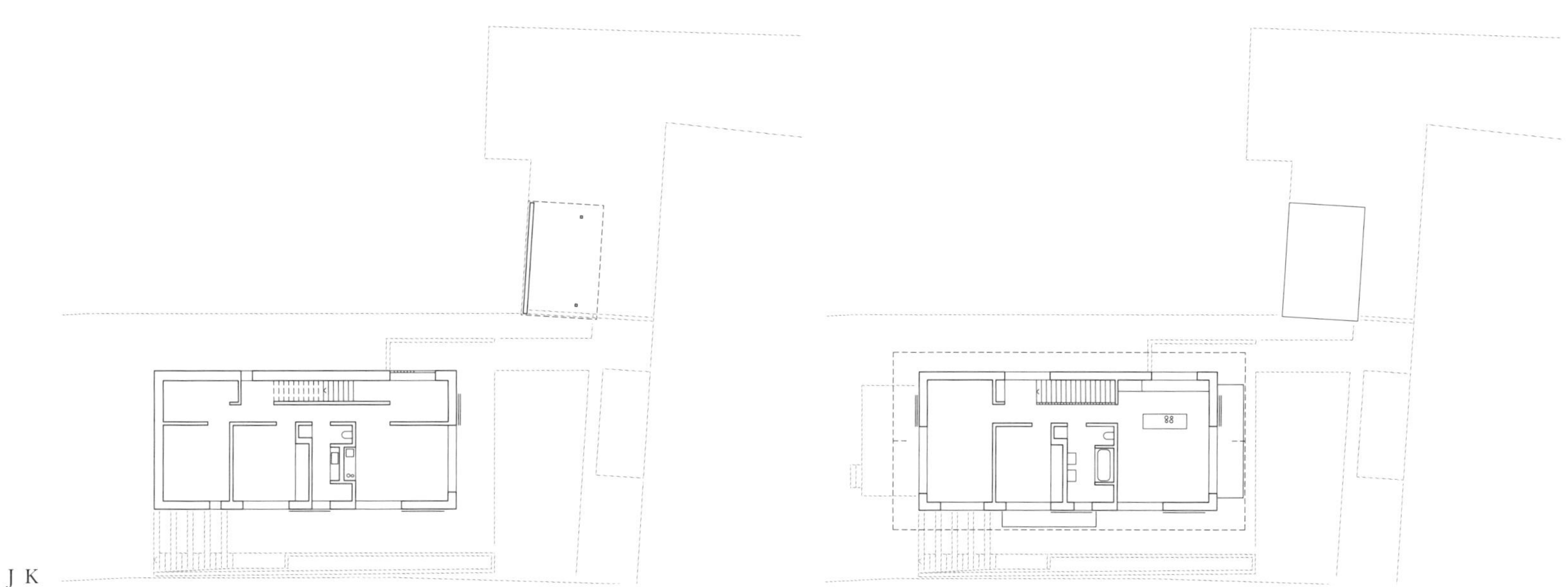

G Entrance area
H First floor hallway
I Bathroom detail
J Ground floor plan
K First floor plan

ZODIAC

A

185 ZODIAC

PALMA DE MALLORCA
SPAIN

AREA
140 m²
YEAR
2021
PHOTOGRAPHY
Arturo + Lauren
www.arturoandlauren.com

Zodiac is a turnkey complete reform project of an exclusive 140-square-meter apartment, located in the quiet residential area of Illetas. Inspired by the light, simplicity and warmth of the Mediterranean, the design focuses on aesthetic beauty and maximum functionality of the space through high quality materials and customized solutions. All the rooms of the house are oriented to the south. At the front line of the bay of Illetas it offers unsurpassed views. The apartment is equipped with large, spacious and very bright rooms, which together with fine materials such as oak and stone make up the integral design of the project. In the living room, curtains frame the view of the open sea. The stage-like presentation of the seating area creates an intimate exchange between inside and outside.

A Seating area with open view to the outside
B Living spaces featuring oak and stone
C Hanging lamps enhance the apartment's warmth

B C

D

E

F

G

D Open standing bathtub
E Bedroom with sea view
F Bathroom
G The window provides an open view of the sea from the bathroom

188

H

I J

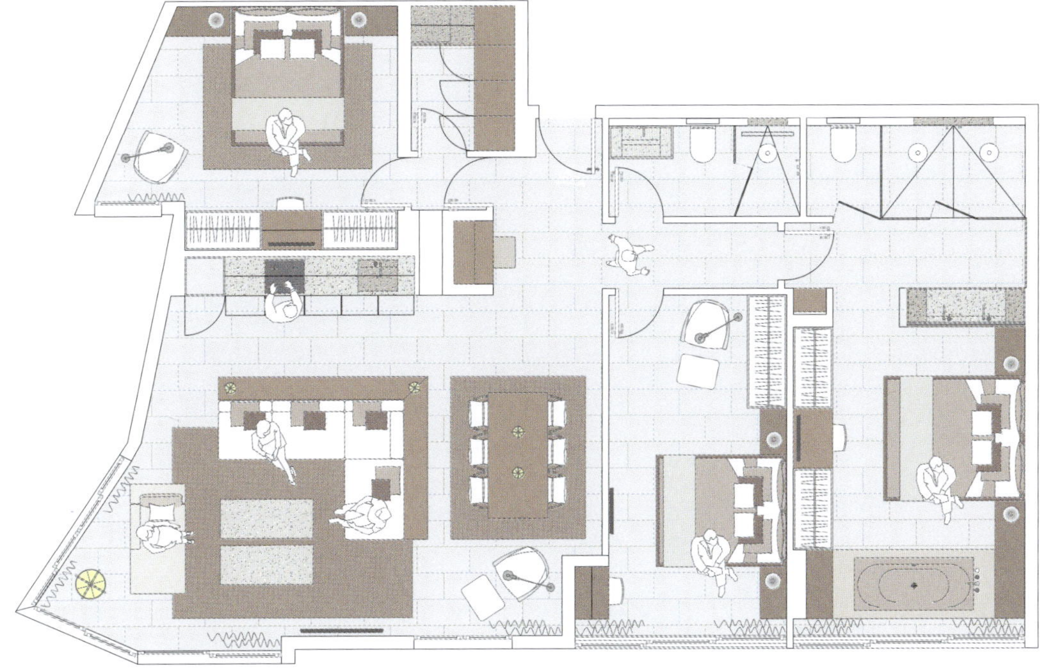

K

H Open living space
I Kitchen detail
J Dining area
K Floor plan

EAST LAKE BEACH HOUSE

A

EAST LAKE BEACH HOUSE

REHOBOTH BEACH
DE, USA

INTERIOR DESIGNER
Baron Gurney Interiors
AREA
1,148 m^2
YEAR
2019
PHOTOGRAPHY
John Cole
www.johncolephoto.com

Located south of downtown Rehoboth Beach lies an unexpected small body of water. Silver Lake forms the western border of the site for this project, a lot which extends east to the Atlantic Ocean. The house design takes advantage of the unique location by highlighting views of both Silver Lake and the Atlantic Ocean and featuring an array of indoor and outdoor spaces. The three-story weekend residence was built for a large family with ample room for entertaining. Composed of four distinct gabled volumes, the perceived size of the house is minimized. Nestled between the gables is a roof deck that feels both intimate and expansive, offering panoramic views of Silver Lake and the Atlantic Ocean. The materials employed are traditional and timeless. Cedar shingles, copper panels, mahogany windows and doors, white oak flooring, and natural stone were all chosen for their durability in a harsh oceanfront environment.

A East façade facing the beach
B Dining and living area with sliding doors leading to screened porch

B

C

D

C Kitchen and dining area organized in horizontal lines
D Covered terrace and swimming pool
E Glassed-in porch ocean view
F Transparent connection of volumes providing lake views through the house

E

F

G

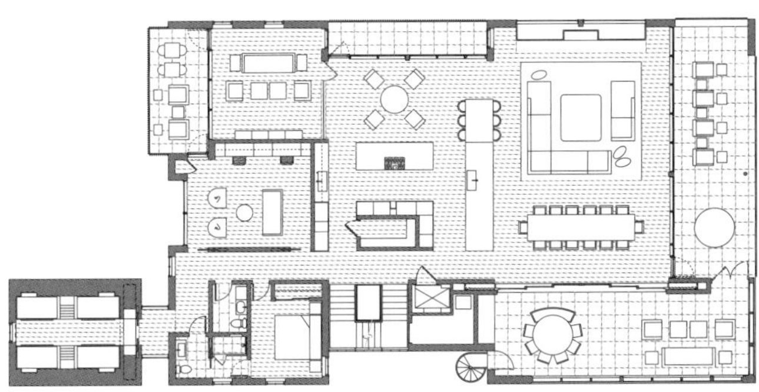

H I

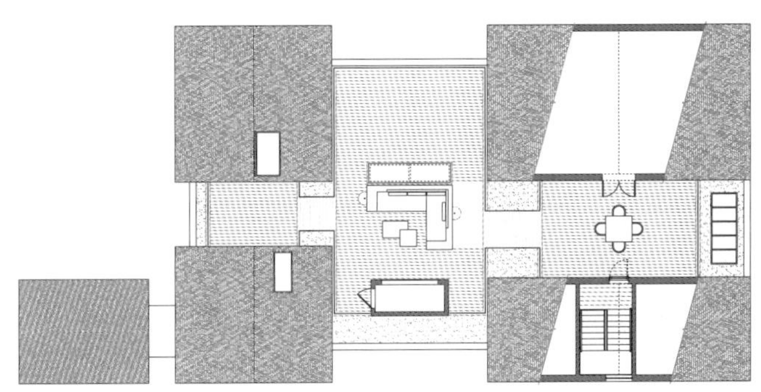

J K

G Three floors of covered terraces overlook a swimming pool, the beach, and ocean
H Ground floor plan
I First floor plan
J Second floor plan
K Roof floor plan

196

CASA EN EL AIRE

A

CASA EN EL AIRE

ZAHARA DE LOS ATUNES
SPAIN

INTERIOR DESIGN
Alfaro Hofmann
AREA
400 m²
YEAR
2023
PHOTOGRAPHY
Fernando Guerra
www.ultimasreportagens.com

Casa en el Aire's design is inspired by its distinctive rocky surroundings, which provide a captivating visual experience at sunrise and sunset. The foundation was constructed with local stone, allowing the structure to rest comfortably on the slope, creating the impression of a floating house. Placed at an optimal height to ensure unobstructed views of the sunset reflection on the Atlantic Ocean, the main living and outdoor spaces on the first floor extend horizontally towards the ocean. On the opposite side, to the south-east, a courtyard has been created to provide tranquility and shelter from Tarifa's strong winds. Here an additional entrance leads to the ground floor with complementary rooms. Connected to the sunrise and landscape to the south-east and the sunset and ocean to the south-west, this residence captures the spectacle of its surroundings while providing privacy to its residents.

A Bird's-eye view of the house
B Terrace and pool during sunset

B

C Open living and dining space

C

D

E F

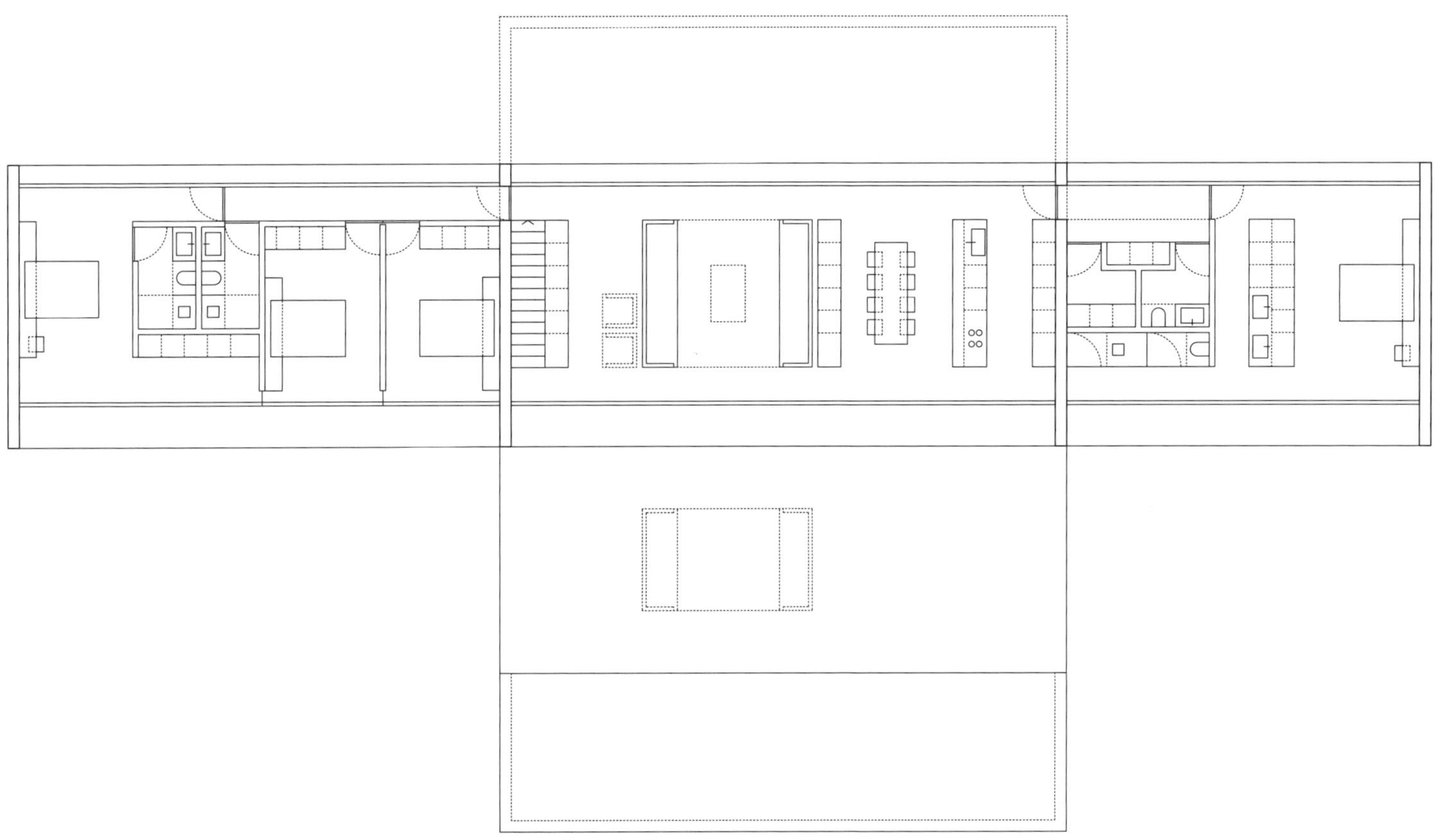

G

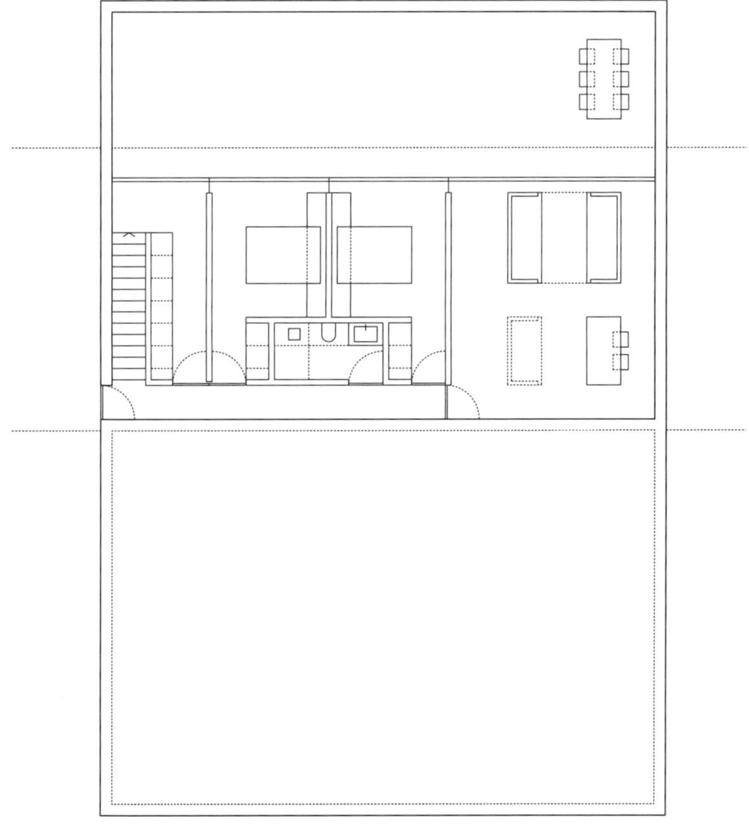

H

D Dining space opening to terrace and pool
E Bathroom sea view
F Bedroom sea view
G First floor plan
H Ground floor plan

PACIFIC HOUSE

A

203 PACIFIC HOUSE

LANDSCAPE DESIGN
Xanthe White Landscape Design
AREA
730 m^2
YEAR
2019
PHOTOGRAPHY
Simon Wilson
www.simonwilson.co.nz

Pacific House is located on the oceanfront north of Auckland in a sand dune setting. The aim was to provide a large vacation home for families and their guests with both communal and private areas. The house is designed as a series of separate pavilions, with glazed connections providing internal access, but also encouraging connections across the outdoor courtyards. While predominantly single level, one pavilion has an upper level guest suite, while another contains media and wellness spaces concealed below grade. The form of the building contrasts the weight of the concrete with expansive glass walls and fine steel-framed sliding doors. The roof is designed in the form of metal prisms, reminiscent of the surrounding sand dunes blown by the wind. A muted palette of exposed concrete, limestone, and bleached oak harmonizes with the sandy driftwood backdrop of the pine forest.

A Bedroom with east terrace
B Exterior view of the entrance looking through the house

B

C

D

C North façade of the living pavilion
D Dining area with view of the sea
E Glass hallway linking the pavilions and garden courtyard

E

F

G

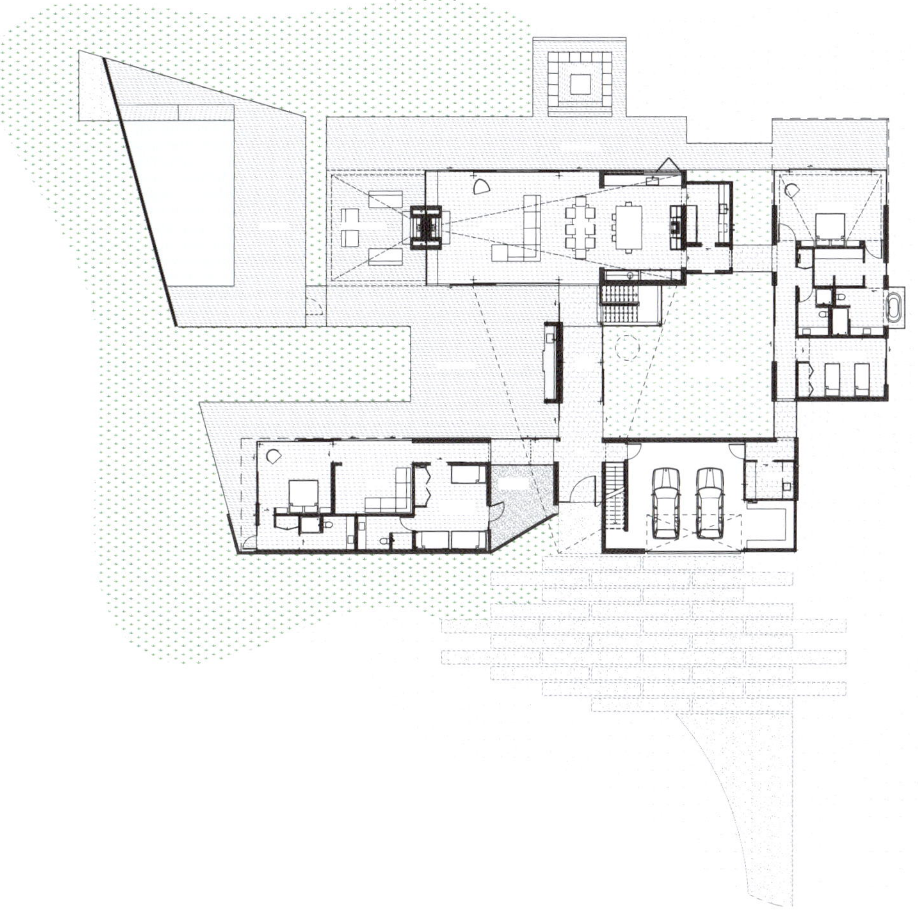

H

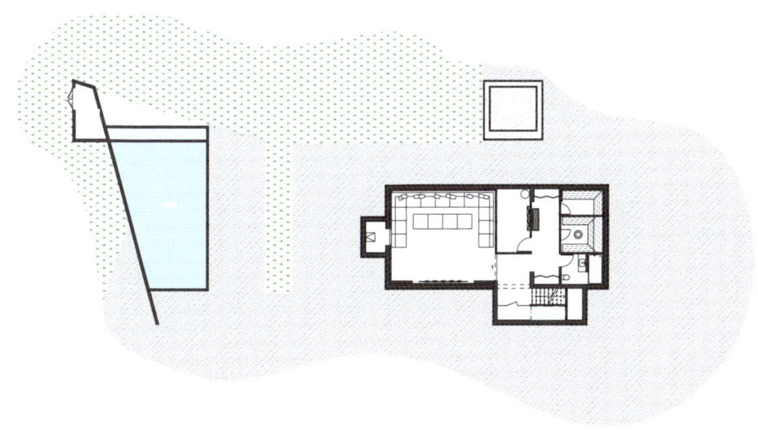

I

F Aerial view
G North terrace
H Ground floor plan
I Lower level plan

208

THE BEACH HOUSE

A

209 THE BEACH HOUSE

VISAKHAPATNAM
INDIA

ARCHITECT
Studio JH
AREA
700 m²
YEAR
2020
PHOTOGRAPHY
Sebastian Zachariah
www.phxindia.com

The interior design of the beach house focuses on letting spaces flow into one another by implementing a cohesive color scheme and making use of materials conducive to the tropical surroundings. Sandstone floors and walls set the overall tone of the house, while being complemented by wood, fabric and cane. Viewed from the front gate, the building is characterized by inconspicuous wooden screens and a blocked-out façade. This does not only provide privacy to residents, but also reveals the site's ocean views as a surprise. After entering through the front door, the double height living area awaits with a grand overlook of the pool deck, infinity pool and ocean. Several small and cozy entertainment areas are sprawled around the house to provide space for relaxation and hangout areas. The beach house features five bedrooms, seven bathrooms, four living areas, a 12-seater dining area and two kitchens.

A Exterior
B Pool deck ocean view

B

C

D

C Dining area
D Top-down view of the living area
E Double height living area opening up to the outside

F

G H

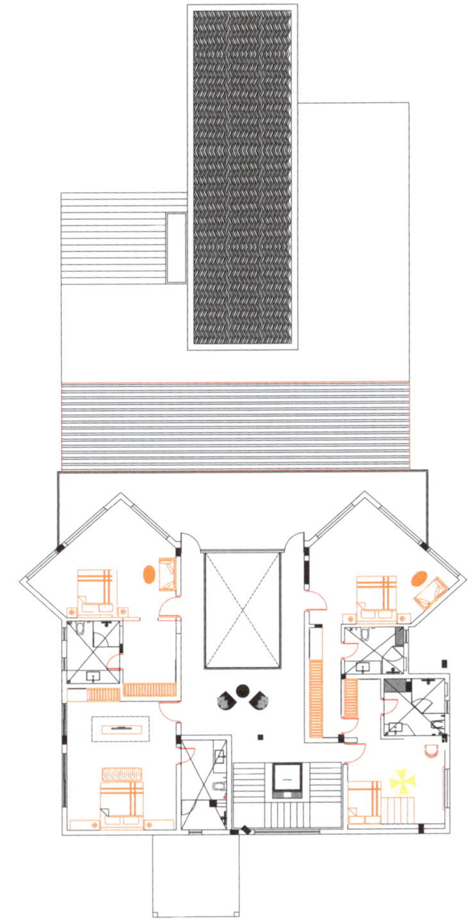

I J

F Master bedroom with access to the top deck
G Bathroom
H Second bedroom
I Ground floor plan
J First floor plan

SKYPOOL VILLA

A

215

SKYPOOL VILLA

KANAGAWA
JAPAN

AREA
473.6 m^2
YEAR
2021
PHOTOGRAPHY
Shinichi Ogawa

The design of Skypool Villa consists of a clear spatial composition that maximizes the impact of the coastal site with sea views to the south and views of Mount Fuji to the north. The house consists of three floors. The south façade is entirely oriented to the sea, with a projecting white volume with terrace and pool extending the space to the sea. On the lower floor, the living and dining area is designed as a semi-outdoor space. Sliding glass doors open the front of the house to the terrace, infinity pool and ocean. A wall height of 4.5 meters and a white minimalist interior design maximizes the impact of the transition to the surrounding nature. The north façade of the house is characterized by a large staircase leading to the rooftop, where an elevated sky pool awaits. The pool, made of transparent acrylic panels, offers an unobstructed panoramic view of the sea in front and Mount Fuji in the distance.

A South façade facing the ocean
B Bird's-eye pool view

B

C Glass sliding doors opening to terrace and infinity pool

C

D

E

SKYPOOL VILLA

KANAGAWA
JAPAN

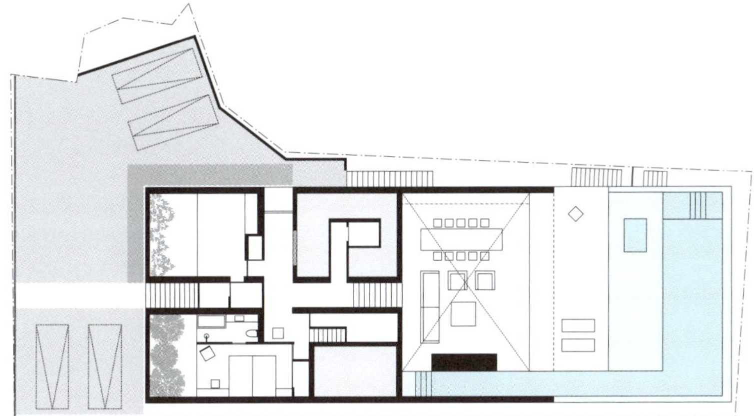

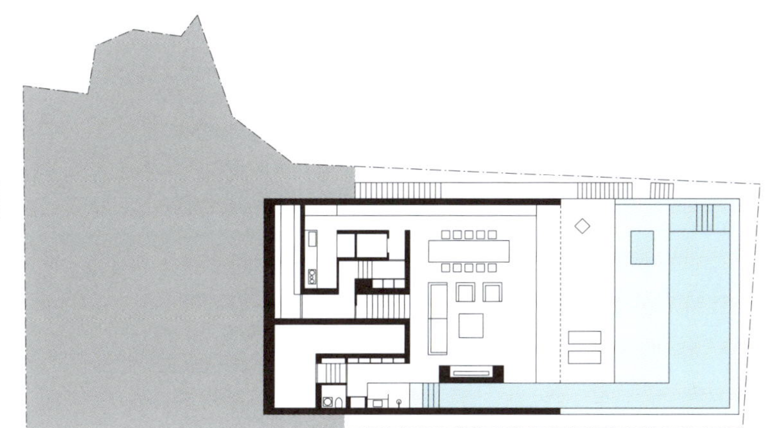

F G

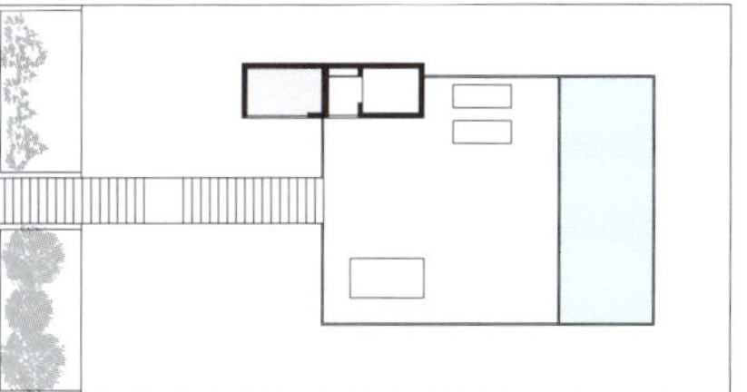

H I

D Rooftop pool during sunset
E Living and dining area sea view
F Lower floor plan
G Ground floor plan
H Upper floor plan
I Rooftop floor plan

A Caspar David Friedrich
The Monk by the Sea, 1808–1810
Oil/canvas
110 cm × 171.5 cm
Alte Nationalgalerie, Berlin

Around 1800, a new view of the landscape emerged in Classicist and Romantic painting. As early as Nicolas Poussin and Claude Lorrain, nature had become a lyrical, ideal subject. Now it became the heroic carrier of social or idyllic carrier of personal longings, nostalgia and aspirations.

A

E

PURAS Architecture
www.puras.dk
Photo Credits
Tina Steffansen
www.studio55.dk
22 — 27

R

Resolution: 4 Architecture
www.re4a.com
Photo Credits
Resolution: 4 Architecture
www.re4a.com
94 — 99

Richard Cole Architecture
www.richardcolearchitecture.com.au
Photo Credits
Simon Wood
www.swphotography.net.au
10 — 15

RTA Studio
www.rtastudio.co.nz
Photo Credits
Patrick Reynolds
118 — 123

S

Shinichi Ogawa & Associates
www.shinichiogawa.com
Photo Credits
Shinichi Ogawa
214 — 219

sw|a sternberg werner architekten
www.sw-a.de
Photo Credits
Kai Sternberg
100 — 105

Amelia Tavella
www.instagram.com/amelia_tavella
Photo Credits
Thibaut Dini
www.thibautdini.co
136 — 141

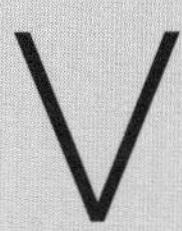

Vaslab Architecture
www.vaslabarchitecture.com
Photo Credits
Ketsiree Wongwan (A), Spaceshift Studio (B, D, E, G, H) www. spaceshiftstudio.com, Wara Suttiwan (C, F)
106 — 111

Architect Ante Vrban
www.antevrban.com
Photo Credits
Architect Ante Vrban www.antevrban.com
70 — 75

Wespi de Meuron Romeo architects
www.wdmra.ch
Photo Credits
Hannes Henz
www.hanneshenz.ch
142 — 147

Wittman Estes
www.wittman-estes.com
Photo Credits
Andrew Pogue
www.andrewpogue.com
52 — 57

XTEN Architecture
www.xtenarchitecture.com
Photo Credits
Art Gray Photography
www. artgrayphoto.com
160 — 165

IMPRINT

The Deutsche Nationalbibliothek lists this publication in the Deutsche Nationalbibliografie; detailed bibliographic data are available on the Internet at http://dnb.dnb.de.

ISBN 978-3-03768-296-8

www.braun–publishing.ch

1st edition 2024

Editor
Editorial Office van Uffelen

Editorial staff and layout
Elena Metzl, Chris van Uffelen

Graphic concept
Eva Finkbeiner

Reproduction
Bild1Druck GmbH, Berlin